The Well-Read Game

Playful Thinking

Jesper Juul, Geoffrey Long, William Uricchio, and Mia Consalvo, editors

The Art of Failure: An Essay on the Pain of Playing Video Games, Jesper Juul, 2013

Uncertainty in Games, Greg Costikyan, 2013

Play Matters, Miguel Sicart, 2014

Works of Game: On the Aesthetics of Games and Art, John Sharp, 2015

How Games Move Us: Emotion by Design, Katherine Isbister, 2016

Playing Smart: On Games, Intelligence, and Artificial Intelligence, Julian Togelius, 2018

Fun, Taste, & Games: An Aesthetics of the Idle, Unproductive, and Otherwise Playful, John Sharp and David Thomas, 2019

Real Games: What's Legitimate and What's Not in Contemporary Video Games, Mia Consalvo and Christopher A. Paul, 2019

Achievement Relocked: Loss Aversion and Game Design, Geoffrey Engelstein, 2020

Play Like a Feminist, Shira Chess, 2020

Ambient Play, Larissa Hjorth and Ingrid Richardson, 2020

Making Games: The Politics and Poetics of Game Creation Tools, Stefan Werning, 2021

Treacherous Play, Marcus Carter, 2022

Repairing Play: A Black Phenomenology, Aaron Trammell, 2023

Player vs. Monster: The Making and Breaking of Video Game Monstrosity, Jaroslav Švelch, 2023

The Stuff Games Are Made Of, Pippin Barr, 2023

Mainstreaming and Game Journalism, David B. Nieborg and Maxwell Foxman, 2023

The Beauty of Games, Frank Lantz, 2023

Run and Jump: The Meaning of the 2D Platformer, Peter McDonald, 2024

The Rule Book: The Building Blocks of Games, Jaakko Stenros and Markus Montola, 2024

The Well-Read Game: On Playing Thoughtfully, Tracy Fullerton and Matthew Farber, 2025

The Well-Read Game

On Playing Thoughtfully

Tracy Fullerton and Matthew Farber

The MIT Press
Cambridge, Massachusetts | London, England

The MIT Press
Massachusetts Institute of Technology
77 Massachusetts Avenue, Cambridge, MA 02139
mitpress.mit.edu

The MIT Press would like to thank the anonymous peer reviewers who provided comments on drafts of this book. The generous work of academic experts is essential for establishing the authority and quality of our publications. We acknowledge with gratitude the contributions of these otherwise uncredited readers.

This book was set in Stone Serif and Stone Sans by Westchester Publishing Services. Printed and bound in the United States of America.

Library of Congress Cataloging-in-Publication Data

Names: Fullerton, Tracy, author. | Farber, Matthew, author.
Title: The well-read game : on playing thoughtfully / Tracy Fullerton and Matthew Farber.
Description: Cambridge, Massachusetts : The MIT Press, 2025. | Series: Playful thinking | Includes bibliographical references and index.
Identifiers: LCCN 2024028463 (print) | LCCN 2024028464 (ebook) | ISBN 9780262552233 (paperback) | ISBN 9780262382915 (epub) | ISBN 9780262382922 (pdf)
Subjects: LCSH: Educational games. | Video games in education. | Reading.
Classification: LCC LB1029.G3 F85 2025 (print) | LCC LB1029.G3 (ebook) | DDC 371.33/7—dc23/eng/20240904
LC record available at https://lccn.loc.gov/2024028463
LC ebook record available at https://lccn.loc.gov/2024028464

10 9 8 7 6 5 4 3 2 1

EU product safety and compliance information contact is: mitp-eu-gpsr@mit.edu

This book is dedicated to Bernie, who gave us permission to play well, and to our students and families, who continue to play deeply and meaningfully with us every day.

Tracy would like to acknowledge her father, who taught her to read joyfully and well, and to imagine and create playfully and thoughtfully.

Matthew would like to acknowledge his mother, who instilled in him a love of reading and gaming, feeding his interests with *Dungeons & Dragons* and *Choose Your Own Adventure* books.

Contents

On Thinking Playfully

Many people (we series editors included) find video games exhilarating, but it can be just as interesting to ponder why that is so. What do video games do? What can they be used for? How do they work? How do they relate to the rest of the world? Why is play both so important and so powerful?

Playful Thinking is a series of short, readable, and argumentative books that share some playfulness and excitement with the games that they are about. Each book in the series is small enough to fit in a backpack or coat pocket, and combines depth with readability for any reader interested in playing more thoughtfully or thinking more playfully. This includes, but is by no means limited to, academics, game makers, and curious players.

So, we are casting our net wide. Each book in our series provides a blend of new insights and interesting arguments with overviews of knowledge from game studies and other areas. You will see this reflected not just in the range of titles in our series, but in the range of authors creating them. Our basic assumption is simple: video games are such a flourishing medium that any new perspective on them is likely to show us something unseen or forgotten, including those from such unconventional voices as artists, philosophers, or specialists in other industries or fields of study. These books are bridge builders, cross-pollinating both areas with new knowledge and new ways of thinking.

At its heart, this is what Playful Thinking is all about: new ways of thinking about games and new ways of using games to think about the rest of the world.

Jesper Juul
Geoffrey Long
William Uricchio
Mia Consalvo

Acknowledgments

We are deeply indebted to the work of Louise Rosenblatt, Perry Nodelman, Bernie DeKoven, Brian Upton, and other scholars and thinkers whose work and ideas we built upon. We would like to thank Jim Erekson, Philip Mayhofer, Brian Upton (again!), Tara McPherson, Sonja Schenk, Navid Khonsari, Chris Floyd, and José Zagal for their generous time and thoughts as we worked through the ideas in this book. We are grateful to Laurence Musgrove, who shared his ability to capture our ideas with a beautiful drawing of what happens when we play. We would also like to thank all the player-response contributors: Grace Collins, Maynard Hearns, Richard Lemarchand, Diego Melendez, Anooj Vadodkar, Youbin Wang, Linhan Li, Andrew Phelps, Farai Halle, Ian Schreiber, Jim Erekson (again!), Bernice Wang, Noah Schwartz, Nicholas Fortugno, and Andrew Goldstein, plus those who asked to remain anonymous. Finally, we'd like to thank MIT Press's Noah J. Springer and the Playful Thinking series editors Jesper Juul, Geoffrey Long, William Uricchio, and Mia Consalvo.

Introduction

> We had this experience where we would play with people and not know who they were and still have a profound connection with them. Toward the end of the game, it suddenly gets really cold and icy, and it becomes really difficult to progress. Eventually, your character sort of gives up, you can't go on any longer, and at that point, my dad and I thought it might have been the end of the game. It was sort of a sad ending until minutes later, the game comes back up and you're at your goal. You're at this beautiful mountaintop filled with all the creatures you've seen in the world below. And it's this beautiful example of the End, and that it doesn't have to be a bad thing. I think that that gave my dad some kind of peace because, near the end of his life, he was playing a game that told him that, in the end, it would be all right. It was a few weeks after he passed that I realized this journey within the game, it reflected the journey I was going on with my dad.
>
> —Sophia Ouellette (2016), fifteen-year-old *Journey* player

This book is about the experiences we have when we play games: not the outcomes of play or the aesthetics of formal game structures themselves, but the ephemeral and emotional experiences of being in play that all players have though rarely discuss. These private stories are what we tell ourselves as we play, the questions we ask, and our reactions to the game's intent. We call these experiences "readings" because they involve so many of the same inherent aspects of engaging with literary, cinematic, and other expressive texts. We do not mean to conflate games with these media or aesthetic forms, only to shine a light on the beauty and importance of player-evoked experiences of being in games and to think about how we may learn to value such experiences when we discuss games beyond their formal aspects. When we think of a game that is experienced in such a way, we call it "well-read" rather than well-played because we want to emphasize the personal, interpretive nature of that experience and the way in which it relates to our reading of texts of all kinds.

We are basing our idea of the "well-read game" on a convergence of literary, media, and play theories: specifically, the works of Louise Rosenblatt's (1938, 1978) *reader-response theory*, Brian Upton's (2017) *situational game theory*, Tracy Fullerton's (2004, 2024) *playcentric design theory*, and Bernie DeKoven's (1978, 2013) *well-played game philosophy*. Each of these theories, from its own perspective, challenges notions of a separate, objective, or authorial meaning in a text and underscores the richness that arises from the varied responses of readers who, in essence, coauthor the meaning of each text through their active engagement with it. Taken together, these theories point to a richer understanding of what a game is and how we might better value our experiences with games to become more thoughtful readers of their essential meanings.

As we discuss in chapter 1, Rosenblatt's reader-response theory establishes the idea that texts—and here, we consider games as multimodal texts—are not complete until they are met with a reader. From this unique transaction between reader and text, emerges a reading. This transaction highlights the diversity of interpretations that can arise as readers bring their individual backgrounds, experiences, and perspectives to the reading experience. In chapters 2 and 3, we explore how the ability to evoke readings that go beyond the mundane facts and rise to the level of an aesthetic experience, to listen to our own emotional experiences as we read (and play), are skills that we can develop if we wish to do so. In chapters 4 and 5, we discuss how a reading can be created by performing our acts of play and by reflecting on that play both during and after the fact. Then, in chapter 6, we talk about what it means to play against an author's intent as we evoke our reading of a game; or, to be in a cultural position where our reading will, by nature of our differing backgrounds to the author's, be oppositional to the intention of the text. And in chapter 7, we examine the multitude of "literary" pleasures that come from reading games as seen from a wide variety of player experiences. Finally, in chapter 8, we discuss what it means to become a "well-read" player of games in a community of other well-read players: how we can look to models from journaling to *play-alouds* and from book clubs to literature circles to enrich our reading of games.

As we explore these ideas, using our own readings of games as well as those of other players, we will be proposing new ways to play—not just to win or to compete but also to savor, to interpret, and to read our experiences in their full essence. Echoing the writers of *The New Games Book* (1976), we believe that how we play a game is more important in the long run than whether we win or lose it. What we mean by this is not the building of expertise but the active listening to one's experience. Learning to play a game masterfully can be a beautiful thing, as we show in our discussions of deep play. But equally beautiful can be playing a game "well," in the sense that Bernie DeKoven describes in *The Well-Played Game: A Player's Philosophy* (1978, 2013). For DeKoven, the word "well" embraces both a state of excellence and of health and wholeness. His insistence that games are experiences created by players and for players, not objects or authorities to sit in judgment of us, permeates the heart of our ideas. His statement that "winning doesn't have to become the goal" informs our sense that there is more to playing than winning or losing. "We have already defined another criterion for playing—that of the experience of playing well together—which transcends any game we are playing. We can define winning as nothing more or less than what happens when the game ends" (DeKoven 2013, 104).

For us, a "well-read" game is one that is played and understood by our whole person—our heart and our mind. In a well-read game, it is not the formal aspects of the system that are of primary interest; rather, it is the player and their experience of that game that makes it whole, makes it real, and makes it worth talking about and reflecting on. Reflecting on the well-read game is like what DeKoven calls the "nineteenth hole"—the place we go after we play to have a drink or snack and to relive the best moments of the game. "We talk about what we can—the moments, the particular plays. That's all we seem to be able to talk about. The game as a whole is too difficult to hold on to. So we talk about the plays. . . . We talk about the times when we were really playing well. We can't let those times go by without savoring them" (DeKoven 2013, 112–113). This ephemeral experience—which only occurs during play and which is fleeting, individual, and difficult to capture—is what we consider to be the jewel of gameplay, the treasure all players seek, whether they realize it or not, and the true raison d'etre of play.

Throughout this book, in keeping with the concept of personal, aesthetic readings, we use first-person passages from the authors and other contributors. In each chapter, both coauthors share readings and journal entries, which serve as examples of "player response," that are then unpacked as we go. The book culminates with submissions from other players in our extended community who have shared their experiences of reading games with us.

In our classrooms, both coauthors invite students to reflect, unpack, and articulate their thoughts after gameplay in game journals. Coauthor Matthew Farber also observed reflective journaling in his study of game-based learning classrooms (2018). We take inspiration from these practices as well as the *reader-response notebook* approach, a decades-old strategy popular in literature classrooms. A reader-response notebook involves readers being taught to jot down their initial impressions of a text, analyze characters, discuss themes, pose questions, and explore their emotional responses to texts (Kesler 2018). These notebooks are not meant to be formal essays or academic analyses; instead, they provide a space for readers to express their subjective experiences with the text and develop a deeper connection with the material. Reader-response notebooks can be particularly valuable in fostering a love of reading, as they encourage readers to actively participate in interpretation and the meaning-making process. We adapt this format by modeling our personal and subjective responses to games, which are also multimodal texts, throughout this book.

Our overarching goal with this book is to begin a dialogue about an aspect of games that is both essential and elusive. When readers of texts realize the extent of the "baggage" they bring with them to the experience, they are better able to respond to the challenges of reading those texts ethically and responsibly. And this is critical for games. Many "expert" and "experienced" players of games do not question their own responses to these experiences. As we see when we discuss how we learn to "read" games as we play them, each player's experience reveals not the game but themselves. And in this revelation, we unveil the potential for discussions to arise—why did this moment of play mean one thing to you and another to me? Rosenblatt and others have characterized reading as a "relationship-building activity" that leads us to an ability to reflect self-critically on the world of a text and, by extension, on the world beyond the text. In this way, Rosenblatt asserts, readers become better citizens of a democratic society. Leaning into this idea, we believe that becoming well-read players can similarly lead us to reflect on our world and become better citizens of it. Rosenblatt argues that our misguided focus on the analysis of the form of texts and the search for "right" answers when understanding them has been a disservice to literature and to readers. Similar to DeKoven's dismissal of "the game" as the primary object of interest, Rosenblatt (1995) states the importance of "improving the individual's capacity to evoke meaning from the text by leading [the reader] to reflect self-critically on this process" (24). In this process, we develop a consciousness of our own preconceptions and prejudices "concerning the situations presented in the work, in contrast to the basic attitudes toward life assumed in the re-recreated work" (Rosenblatt 1995, 109). In other words, our response to a work reveals . . . ourselves.

In his article "What Happens When We Read: Picturing a Reader's Responsibilities" (2005), English professor Laurence Musgrove describes asking his students to draw their ideas of what happens when they read a book. From those drawings, Musgrove created a composite image that shows the relationship between the reader, the text, and the response (see figure 0.1). In turn, we worked with Musgrove to draw a similar representation of what we think happens when we read a game. As in the original drawing, we show the relationship between the player, the game, and the response (see figure 0.2). These entities are not entirely separate. In many ways,

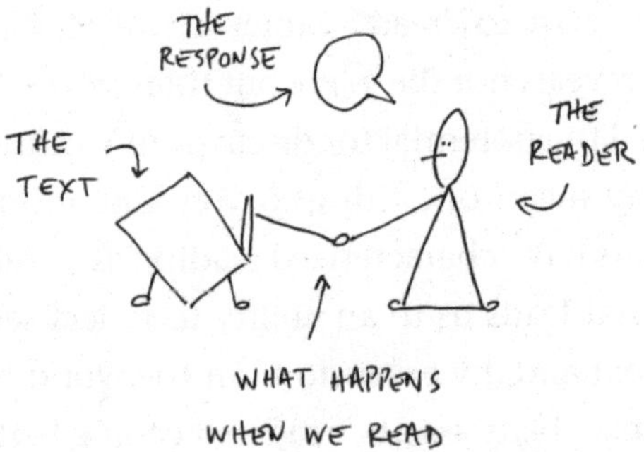

Figure 0.1
"What Happens When We Read." Image by Laurence Musgrove.

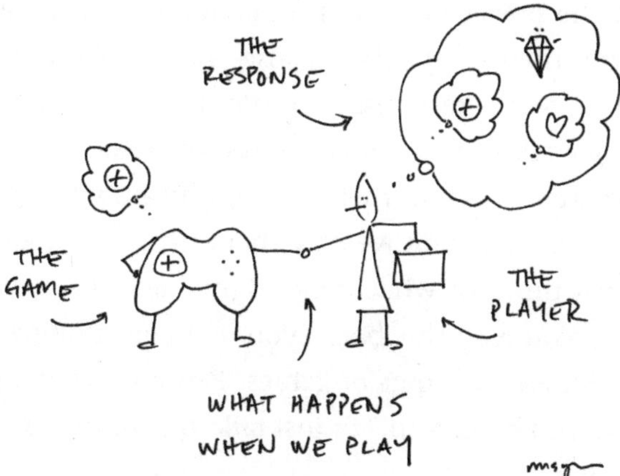

Figure 0.2
"What Happens When We Play." Image by Laurence Musgrove from concepts by Tracy Fullerton and Matthew Farber.

there is no game without a player. A "game" is an inert and abstract object—a collection of items and ideas, or lines of software code—that does nothing and means nothing without a player. As we see when we discuss Upton's (2017) situational game theory, this image depicts the game and its language of play as being part of the player's experience. This is because the game as read is, to a great extent, a manifestation of the player's imagination. Beyond what the game brings to the "conversation," however, lie the emotions and responses of the player, what we believe to be the true treasures of gameplay. As with the reader's response to a written text, the player's response to a game (or "evocation" of it, to use Rosenblatt's term) is created from an amalgam of all our individual prior experiences (our "baggage") as well as from our interactions with the game as designed and experienced.

As authors, we bring our own baggage to this book as well. As a designer and educator, Fullerton brings her desire to see games become more understood and valued as an aesthetic form. As an educator and theorist, Farber brings his hope for more people to understand the power of play and playfulness. Together, we have developed this theory of *player response*—basing our terminology on the concept of reader response—for the thoughtful appreciation of games in hopes that it can advance the discussion around games, why they matter as an aesthetic form, and how we might better articulate that value when we play them, when we speak of them, and when we think of what they might mean to our future. We hope that, as you read this book, you will play along and develop your own aesthetic readings of games. Perhaps begin a game journal, start a game "book club," or just talk to your friends or children about their play.

If you're ready to begin reading games, well, let's start with a poem . . .

1
Reading Games Aesthetically

'Twas brillig, and the slithy toves
Did gyre and gimble in the wabe;
All mimsy were the borogoves,
And the mome raths outgrabe.

—Lewis Carroll, "Jabberwocky"

Reading these words from Lewis Carroll's poem "Jabberwocky" in Through the Looking Glass (1871, 134) makes us feel like we understand something about the world the author is describing. We recognize linguistic markers and devices such as word order, word endings, and parts of speech, and even though many of the words themselves are nonsensical, they still feel like words, and even more than that, they communicate a sense of a place, time, and things happening that we may connect to our own experiences. When we read this poem, as when we read any text, we bring with us our understanding of language, how it works, our vocabulary, our history of reading other texts, as well as our understanding of the world outside texts, and our imagination about things real and imagined. Our encounter with a text is a potpourri of things both intellectual and emotional, immediate and recalled. This assemblage of ideas, connections, and being that a reader brings to any encounter with a text creates what literature scholar Louise Rosenblatt (1978) calls an *event* of reading, an *evoking* of a text by a reader. This event is an experience unique to a reader, unique even to a single moment in a reader's life. And, when a reader pays attention to the "associations, feelings, attitudes, and ideas that these words and their referents arouse within [the reader]," they are creating what Rosenblatt (1978) calls an *aesthetic reading* (25). Rosenblatt writes, "'Listening to' [themself], [the reader] synthesizes these elements into a meaningful structure. *In aesthetic reading, the reader's attention is centered directly on what [they are] living through during [their] relationship with that particular text*" (1978, 25).

Rosenblatt's theories of literary experience, which we return to throughout this book, are deeply influenced by the writings of American educator and philosopher John Dewey, specifically *Art as Experience*, in which Dewey (1934) argues for an understanding of art as a composed *experience* "perceived" by a beholder (35). This understanding of art as based in experience rather than in objects is foundational to Rosenblatt's work, and by extension, to our own theories presented here. As Dewey states, "To perceive, a beholder must create [their] own experience" (54). When we step out of the realm of ordinary experience and into that of the aesthetic, we take on the stance of an active cocreator of such experiences as well as that of a participant in the social process of understanding and valuing works of art across a variety of media. When coauthor Fullerton did a personal aesthetic reading of "Jabberwocky," this was her experience:

> When I read these words, I think of a beautiful summer evening, a "brillig" evening, with the sounds and sights of magical creatures: "slithy toves" that are dancing, perhaps singing, with moonlight sparkling on their "slithy" skin, as they "gyre and gimble" in the quiet, marshy meadow, the "wabe," where I stand and watch.

> A lovely tipsiness pervades the scene, "all mimsy," like me, with birdlike "borogoves" chattering and cooing in the trees, and large, scaley opossum-like "mome raths" curled into their logs, asleep.

Fullerton's feelings about these words have been influenced by the many times she's read them or had them read to her. She says of the reading above, "My imagery comes from personal experiences in real-world forests and imaginary experiences in fictional worlds. It springs from the collision of these personal thoughts and memories with my knowledge of language, how it works, how it makes meaning and the process of comprehension and interpretation I go through when I interact with language. Because I am reading them in a literary work, Carroll's *Through the Looking-Glass* (1871), the sequel to *Alice's Adventures in Wonderland* (1865), my approach to these words is not to find literal, actionable meaning in them. I've been signaled by the larger context of the text to expect absurdity and to seek out enjoyment from that absurdity. And so, whereas my imagination has provided imagery of natural, if magical, beauty and mapped that imagery to emotional sensibilities—a calm and serene evening—it is only my own interpretation."

Having done their own aesthetic reading of the passage, a reader could discuss their interpretation with friends and might find interesting differences in their experiences of these classic lines of a well-known literary text. They might track down the etymological history of these made-up words to see if the author intended some secret meaning, seeking, like detectives, to understand more about the passage beyond their own imaginings. As they explore and interpret, they might wonder about the very nature of language and communication itself: about how and why meaning is made, by and between people, over time, and across communities of thought. Each of these activities would lead to new readings of the text, and all of this from a simple play of language. Carroll's text is in fact a gamelike poem meant to spark our minds with its silliness and lead us into a literal "wonderland"—a state of wonder.

Rosenblatt's (1986) concept of the aesthetic reading of texts is a core concept in literary *transactional theory*, which proposes that the act of reading is a transaction between a reader and a text that evokes a particular experience and meaning for that reader, a *lived experience*, which is the essence of our emotional lives as readers. Most of us have such experiences, of course, not only while reading but while looking at art, while watching film, while walking in the woods, or even just strolling down the street. We live in a constant stream of thoughts and ideas that we let pass over us, sometimes explored but mostly unacknowledged. As Dewey (1934) says of the ordinary world, "Things are experienced but not in such a way that they are composed into *an* experience. There is distraction and dispersion" (35). When we actively engage with these thoughts, however, and capture them by writing in journals, discussions, or by thinking aloud, we create the basis for aesthetic readings. By reading, we mean this act of thoughtful interpretation and understanding, which can be associated with written text, of course, but also with visual, aural, and other sensory arts and experiences. The act of reading multimodal experiences such as film, theater, music, and—importantly for our discussion—games can be done for many reasons, which include pleasure and growth. But to engage with the full range of pleasures a text offers, we must be literate in the ways that that text is communicating with us. And if we are literate and able to read a text, we still must be actively listening to our own responses as we engage with it. Importantly, we must be listening for more than just information. We must listen to our emotional and aesthetic responses as well.

In transactional theory, aesthetic reading is set in contrast to *efferent reading*, where the reader's attention is focused primarily on the information to be acquired and used later. When we read street signs or tax forms, we are reading efferently. You are likely reading this book efferently right now. Efferent reading is characterized by its utility. We read efferently to learn something, possibly so we can do something. When we read the instructions for a game, we are reading efferently because we need to know how the game works in order to play it. When we read the instructions for our new refrigerator, we are also reading efferently. We can read a novel efferently, and we will learn how the characters did what they did but we may not understand why. A novel like *The Great Gatsby* (Fitzgerald 1925), though it has information in it that we can read efferently, is best read when we listen to the language, visualize the settings and the characters, and follow the flow of its fateful themes. Trying to read "Jabberwocky" for useful information, however, would be a nonsensical experience because it has been written to be read only from an aesthetic stance. "Jabberwocky" is a text that is meant to intentionally play with language and our process of making meaning from it. It sits within a history of literature about language play and the creation of meaning and is meant to taunt and confound us with that process by holding its meaning just outside the possibilities of our understanding (Bohman-Kalaja 2007). As such, it helps us to see more clearly the way in which the interaction of a reader of any text and the text itself is an event from which meaning can be constructed.

But beyond the extreme of this nonsense poem lies the vast majority of literary works, which can be read across the complexities of a continuum between the efferent and the aesthetic. Take Shakespeare's *Romeo and Juliet* as an example. Read efferently, in a CliffsNotes version, we have mere information: Two families are feuding, but their children fall in love. Rather than be parted, the lovers choose suicide. The tragedy provokes a nebulous truce between their families, which amounts to a sad news story at best when read efferently. However, when read aesthetically, we have the beauty of the language, the longing of the lovers, the dangerous, sparkling meeting at the party, the violent folly of the fight and murder, the desperate need that drives the lovers' deceptive death play, and the misunderstanding that brings true tragedy. The characters are recognizable to us, even hundreds of years after their writing. The situation rings true with the pain of prejudice, and communities separated by a history of blood feuds. The violence shocks us but is also sadly recognizable. We can bring our own experiences, our own understandings to this text, evoking as we read or watch a unique aesthetic interpretation of this literary experience. And, as with "Jabberwocky," we can discuss and debate our personal interpretation of this text, finding key similarities and differences in our varying experiences. Sharing our lived experiences as readers can make us a part of many overlapping communities of readers—communities that can cross time, distance, culture, gender, and even language.

This is the essence of the literary experience, the reason that we engage with literary texts of all kinds. The combined act of aesthetic reading and learning what others have made of a text, to compare one's relationship to it with that of other readers, "clarifies and crystallizes" our sense of a work, as Rosenblatt suggests (1978, 146). The aesthetic reader "likes to hear others' views. Through such interchange, [the reader] can discover how people bringing different temperaments, different literary and life experiences to the texts have engaged in very different transactions with it" (146). On the other hand, the efferent reader who only engages with a text to receive the most basic information from it, and is not engaging with it from an aesthetic stance, will retain only the most fundamental knowledge, if that, from the experience of reading.

Why does this matter to us? And how does it affect our understanding of how video games might be considered experiences of readerly interest? Mariam Karis Cronin (2014) of the National Council of Teachers of English writes eloquently on the distinction between the experience of literature and the basics of literacy—including the stakes for us as a society in valuing the impact of literature on us as readers, stating,

> [Literature] is cerebral and visceral—explicit and implicit. It thrives on ambiguity and nuance. It requires the reader and the writer to have profound insight into the human condition and to be able to comprehend and/or convey those ideas with skill and imagination.

> Literature—both the production and the interpretation of it—requires the writer and the reader to have excellent literacy skills to access and/or produce text that, as Ray Bradbury wrote, has "pores." Although literacy is the basis for literature, a society that promotes only transactional, foundational literacy at the expense of the literacy skills literature demands would be shallow and dispassionate—one that promotes paint-by-number illustrations at the expense of a Sistine Chapel. Although today the text in question and the medium used may take many forms, 21st-century literacy is a set of complex skills that students need to master to fully understand sophisticated literary texts. After all, if the student does not have the prerequisite skills to read the text or respond to the prompt we assign, then the distinction between literacy and literature is moot. (46)

As Cronin hints at, today's requirements for literacy extend beyond written texts to visual, aural, and interactive media, including video games. Similarly, today's literature extends beyond written texts to include that same range of media and aesthetic forms. Linguist and games scholar James Paul Gee (2007) describes game design as being "made up of images, actions, words, sounds, and movements—that communicates to players because players (conventionally) interpret aspects of that design to have certain meanings" (135). Thus, as we respond to various types of texts—written or playable—we engage in processes of meaning-making described as an "event" between a reader and a text. Whether that event is between a reader and a film, a reader and a poem, or a reader and a game, there is the opportunity for meaning to be made, shared, and valued. This kind of personal and social meaning-making is core to both Dewey's and Rosenblatt's vision of how aesthetic experience and education sit at the heart of a democratic society (Faust 2000, 29).

Most literary texts, unlike a nonsense poem like "Jabberwocky," rely on the reader's ability to understand both the basic facts of a story, as in our CliffsNotes version of *Romeo and Juliet*, and their capacity to engage with that story on an aesthetic basis. Literary texts expect readers to not only comprehend what happens but also to interpret it and situate it within their imagination and worldview. However, only the process of reading aesthetically can make a text truly meaningful for the reader. Without it, a reader is simply going through the motions of word-by-word comprehension. As Cronin suggests above, this basic type of literacy is important but not the end of the story for twenty-first-century readers. Rather, today's readers must engage with efferent and aesthetic readings of texts in *many forms and mediums*. We are proposing here that one form of sophisticated literary text that should be counted among those many forms and mediums is video games. As we demonstrate, games, when read aesthetically, can provide the same level of "profound insight into the human condition" as any other piece of literature or expressive media (Cronin 2014, 26). Learning to read games well, in this case, would seem to be as urgent as learning to read books, journalism, films, poems, and all other forms of art, expression, and communication.

Situating Our Approach

Our approach to understanding how games can be read aesthetically is built upon several foundational theories across game studies and literary theory, which, like Rosenblatt, we return to throughout this book. These theories include Upton's (2017) concept of *situational game design* (see figure 1.1), in which he defines a "player-centric approach" to game theory, similar to Fullerton's playcentric design (2004, 2024). Both Upton and Fullerton are hybrid game designer-theorists, and each has a particular interest in the way that games are developed and received by players. In their separate writings, Upton and Fullerton both shift the focus of game analysis from the game as a system, separate from the player, to the integrated experience of the player and the game. Or, as Upton (2017) writes, "In situational design, the nexus of play lies not in the interface between the player

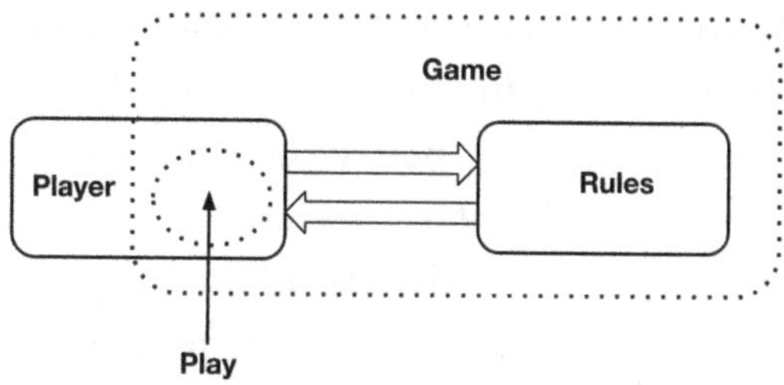

Figure 1.1
Situational game design. Source: Brian Upton.

and the game, but inside the player's mind. Some of the moves the player makes will affect the external state of the game, but others will affect their internal understanding of the game or even their understanding of themselves and the world at large" (6).

Our understanding of games as a phenomenological experience sits in contrast to a common metaphor in game studies, which is to describe games as systems that are separate from the player but in conversation with them. This understanding of games dates back to Chris Crawford's (2000) initial description of the two-way "conversation" between designer and player (6–7) and continues with Mechanics, Dynamics, Aesthetics (MDA), the widely cited theory from Hunicke, Le Blanc, and Zubeck (2004), which also applies cybernetics to describe the transactional nature of that relationship. This cybernetic view of the transactional relationship—which includes, of course, the opportunity for player input and effect on the game system—is generally understood to be the defining quality of interactive experiences. The focus in this understanding of games is on transactions that are related to the input to, and output from, the game system (e.g., choices the player makes), with only limited attention to the player's lived experience within the game and their response to that experience. The metaphor of the game as a system is a useful one, of course, which Fullerton has used as well in *Game Design Workshop* (2004, 2024), and it is one that has entered our vocabulary as a core value that games can bring to learning—systems thinking is a twenty-first-century skill. It is understood that by playing a game system and coming to understand how it works, twenty-first-century learners may be better prepared to understand and interact with real-world complex systems.

However, this hyperfocus on systems thinking is only one way of valuing the player experience. We are proposing an approach that shifts attention from the game system to the *event* of gameplay between a unique player and the game. This is more in line with what play theorist Brian Sutton-Smith (1997) refers to as the *rhetoric of self,* a focus on the subjectivity of the individual at play, "the feelings and meanings of play for the individual player" (192), and also with the ideas of Bernie DeKoven's (1978, 2013) *The Well-Played Game*. DeKoven's philosophy, which concentrates on how a player is thinking and feeling about a game rather than on the game itself, is another that we return to throughout this book. Historically intertwined with DeKoven's participation in the New Games Foundation, an organization and community that promoted player creation and adaptation of games, this philosophy points us toward an approach where what twenty-first-century learners take away from a game is not primarily systems thinking but, even more importantly, a holistic sense of wellness based on a self-awareness of players as individuals who are part of a play community. For DeKoven, what defines a "well-played" game is not "determined by who wins, nor by what game we play, but rather by the *quality* of playing that we have been able to create together" (DeKoven 2013, 28). Based on the merger of Upton's and Fullerton's situational and player-centric theories with Rosenblatt's transactional theory and DeKoven's emphasis on the player's experience of the game rather than simply the game itself, our player-centric model of reading games creates the potential for valuing games as lived, interpreted experiences situated within a community of play. As Upton (2017) describes, the designer creates the *game as designed,* whereas the *game as experienced* is how that design plays out in any particular session, and the *game as understood* is the player's personal grasp of the game, "their mental model of its rules, consequences, meanings, and *more*" (17). *More* for us includes the player's interpretation of the game, their personal and emotional responses to the entire situation and event of play, and the way they are able to express that response within the safety of a supportive community of play.

When we combine a player-centric, situational approach to games with Rosenblatt's transactional theory and Dewey's art as experience, we find a significant overlap. Transactional theory, which has been applied not only to literary criticism and the teaching of literature but also to media such as film (Bordwell 1989) and music (Hoyt 1985), suggests "a reciprocal, mutually defining relationship" between the reader and the literary text (Rosenblatt 1986, 122). Often referred to as *reader-response theory*, in reference to that relationship, an emphasis on the individual cognitive and emotional process of meaning-making in response to media has been taken up widely in literature classrooms at all levels of instruction as a method of increasing student engagement with reading. Although the application of such methods has invited critiques that it espouses an anarchic subjectivism and ignores authorial intent, the underlying theories seem particularly applicable to the understanding of games, given their inherently participatory nature. The tension between authorial and intent and subjective experience, when applied to the reading of games, seems to be an essential component of the two-way interaction between text and reader, rather than a point of contention. This interaction results in a unique experience specific to that reader (or player), that text (or game), at that time and situation. It is an experience, in the sense that Dewey suggests, that can be understood, discussed, and interpreted (Rosenblatt 1938, 1978, 1986). By thus building on player-centric and situational design, as well as transactional theory and reader response, we are able to understand the player's personal and emotional responses to the game as played as a lived experience, what Rosenblatt (1978) refers to as an active process, an "event in the life of a reader" (16). We can see that the same type of mutually defining relationship as is found in reading is also found in the interaction between a player and a game, resulting in a unique play experience that, as Rosenblatt describes in regard to reading, evokes a "shimmering interplay of meanings, associations, feeling-tones" (1978, 54). So, as transactional theory raises the level of reading a literary work to a "creative adventure" (Rosenblatt 1978, 52), so, too, does our theory of thoughtful player response to "a well-read game" raise the bar on expectations of what can be understood from our interactions with a game when framed as an aesthetic experience.

Much like the way that play philosopher Bernard Suits's (1978) *lusory attitude* defines a necessary psychological mindset for play, aesthetic reading of a game also requires adopting a particular relationship to the game as one plays, what is called an *aesthetic stance* or attitude. Similarly, Rosenblatt (1978) observes, "sensing, feeling, imagining, thinking, synthesizing the states of mind, the reader who adopts the aesthetic attitude feels no compulsion other than to apprehend what goes on during this process, to concentrate on the complex structure of experience that [they are] shaping and that becomes for [them] the poem, the story, the play symbolized by the text" (26). By applying this transactional theory to games, we propose a distinctly different relationship, one that focuses on their potential as multimodal texts that can engage players in exploring games deeply and personally, as we see in the following chapters. We can, as we propose in this book, define a transactional player-response theory of gameplay for players that is player-centric and that offers a new, readerly approach to playing games well.

But, first, an example.

Reading a Game: *Unpacking*

In the same manner that we looked at the first few lines of "Jabberwocky" above, we can also demonstrate the potential of a game to be "well-read." The game that we will look at, in some ways, cannot be understood without an aesthetic reading. So, like "Jabberwocky," it proves our point, perhaps too easily. In the following chapters, however, we look at readings of a number of other games and involving different players; many of those texts sit on that spectrum of efferent versus aesthetic texts and will prove to be more complex and interesting examples, with the possibility for varying readings depending on the player's background, life experiences, and the situation of play.

The game that we will look at here, *Unpacking* (Witch Beam 2022), is very simple from a systemic point of view, and if we allow ourselves to play it efferently—that is, without much aesthetic interpretation—it is barely an experience at all. At the start of each level, we are presented with a room, or set of rooms, and a set of boxes (see figure 1.2). We click on boxes to reveal items that are stored within them. Then we click to place the items in the rooms. We do this over and over until we have placed all the items. Then

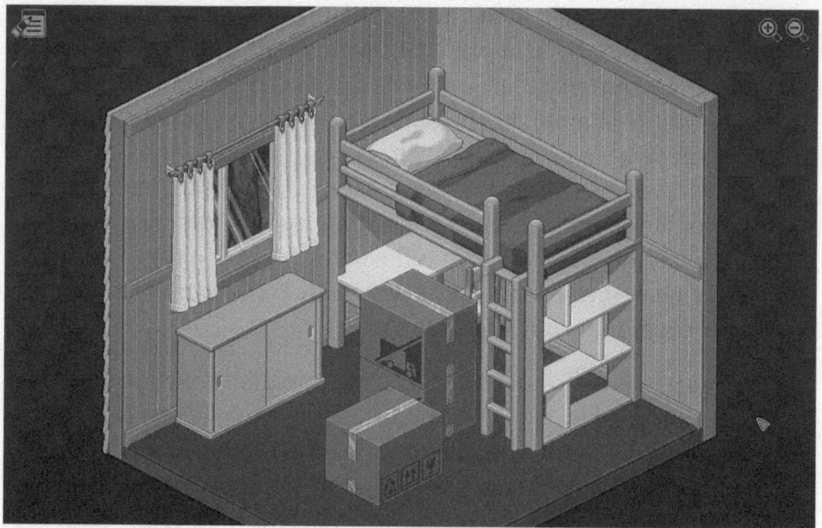

Figure 1.2
Packed boxes from the game *Unpacking*.

the game is over. Like our CliffsNotes version of *Romeo and Juliet*, this is hardly worth discussing. If we take our reading one step further to participate in the metaphor of the game, we understand that the clicking and placing is, as the title suggests, a representation of "unpacking," and the rooms and houses represent the stages of a character's life, from their very first room alone to college, to living with roommates, lovers, and finally building a permanent home for their family. Still, is this much to speak about? Can we read this game with an aesthetic stance?

When Fullerton played the game, she journaled the following:

> I immediately find it nostalgic. The first level is set in 1997, and I recognize the iconic toys in the character's room: a Tamagotchi and a Game Boy, for example. I am not certain about the character's gender, but I guess maybe they are a girl. She likes art and has a lot of art supplies. And she likes gaming, both physical and digital. She has board games and a soccer ball along with her Game Boy. Everything in her room is colorful and upbeat. She seems like a happy kid. She has a journal, so she may be a bit introspective, too. I try making her room messy, putting all her toys on the floor, but the game highlights them in red. So I realize that there is a bit of constraint here; though I can place the toys in creative ways around the room, I can't just toss them on the floor. I feel like that is an interesting choice—almost like the game is enforcing her parents' rules about keeping your room clean! After I've unpacked everything in the first level and put the toys away, I see a picture of my/her room in my photo album (see figure 1.3) with a caption from the character, "Finally, my own room!" It is the tiniest bit of narrative, but I feel like I have helped this young person establish themselves and their identity in their first private space.
>
> The game goes on to later levels, and the unpacking continues. At the start of every level, I'm faced with a mountain of boxes and an empty space to fill with her stuff. I start to see the same stuff over and over and I know where it goes now. It almost begins to feel like my own stuff; it is so recognizable. My character is obviously one who hangs on to childhood things and I keep unpacking the stuffed animals, including a clearly loved stuffed pig, well into adulthood.

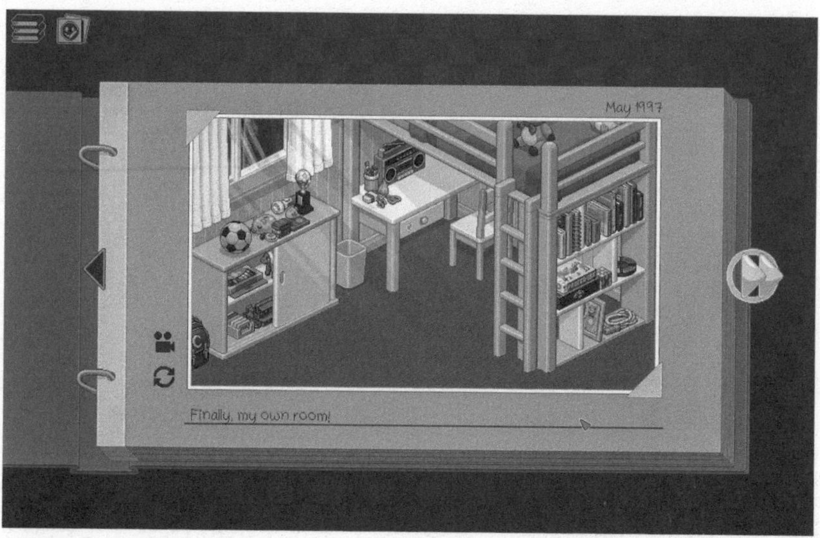

Figure 1.3
Photo album from *Unpacking*.

That pig, and the rest of the brightly colored stuff, becomes her trademark in the spaces she shares, first with roommates and then with a boyfriend who apparently wears and likes only black and gray (see figure 1.4). The "boyfriend level" is a challenge from the outset. She has boxes filled with games, and those go well with his games. But she also has a bunch of brightly colored clothes, underwear, shoes, and so on that just won't fit in his closet and drawers. He hasn't even moved any of his stuff to make room for hers! His apartment is full of his own stuff, and just trying to find some kind of niche to place her colorful, joyful things is a challenge. I sense a disaster in this relationship from the outset. What made her think she should move in with him? This level is so hard because, though I can tidy up his closet and make room for her clothes, you can't move his wall hangings. It seems like he is pretty particular about his art, and so, no matter how hard I try, there is no place for me to hang up her diploma. In the end, I have to shove that under the bed to finish unpacking this level. This is one of the most dramatic, unfortunate moments in the character's life so far. When I put that diploma under the bed, I just feel so bad for her. I know she doesn't belong here.

Figure 1.4
Boyfriend level from the game *Unpacking*.

From this reading of the first few levels of *Unpacking*, we can see a character developing and changing, facing the small but poignant challenges of a life. The system of this game is extremely simple, but as a multimodal text it evokes deep feelings in the player. A connection builds between our character and ourselves as we unpack their lives over and over, trying to help them fit in and finally belong somewhere. Our initial nostalgia for their recognizable items becomes care and concern for the specific items they carry with them in their lives. We can think about the items in our own lives that we cherish and why. What items will we always carry with us? What do they say about us? What special items will we pass on to our children? What stories will we tell them about these special things? *Unpacking* is telling us a story because we are noticing it, interpreting it, and bringing our own experiences to it. If we *don't* notice, if we *don't* interpret, then there is no story; there is only unpacking item after item after item. In this way, as already noted, it is a game that invites an aesthetic reading over a purely efferent one. When Farber played the game with his son, the two were able to discuss some of the objects that his son, eleven years old at the time, did not recognize. It became a lovely intergenerational opportunity to talk about the character that was emerging, where they lived, and why they might have different objects in their home. Farber journaled their experience:

> "The bedroom looks a little bit like yours," I comment to my son, who is the one actually playing the game. I am sitting next to him on the couch, making suggestions as he plays. We recently moved multiple times when I took a professorship opportunity across the country, first to an apartment, then to a house. I watch as he methodically clicks the boxes and then puts items in drawers, shelves, and closets, as he did in his own bedroom. As we play more, he remarks to me that each room seems to have one item that does not belong, like a computer keyboard mixed in with kitchen spices. "That didn't happen when we moved," he says. "Mom labeled all of the boxes by room!" As he continues to unbox and unpack, my mind wanders; I think about the unwitting trauma that my career opportunity may have inflicted on my family, who had to pack and move. In my childhood, we never moved. I always went to the same school and woke up in the same bedroom. My son has moved twice already, each time to a new bedroom, a different neighborhood, another school. As he unpacks, we hope that he, too, unboxes a better life.

Suffice it to say that it is not the systemic aspects of this game that bring value to this experience. It is the potential for aesthetic reading, for the player to experience Rosenblatt's "shimmering interplay of meanings, associations, feeling-tones" in a mutually defining relationship found in the interaction between a player and a game, just as we might find between the reader and the literary text (1978, 54).

Precedents and Potentials

There is a small but emerging set of scholarly works applying reader-response theory with games. For instance, literacy professor April Sanders (2013) conducted a case study of fifteen participants examining three mainstream multiplayer games: *Halo* (Bungee 2001), *World of Warcraft* (Blizzard 2004–), and *The Sims FreePlay* (EA Mobile 2011). An overarching theme that emerged was feelings of living through virtual experiences. One participant recalled memories from childhood as she explored *World of Warcraft*, recalling "fairy tales she read and enjoyed as a young child" (96). Another spoke of how playing *World of Warcraft* "helped them survive a bad roommate situation with a former friend" (96). *Halo* players recalled playing the game with close-knit groups of friends or siblings. One noted, "I almost always think of good times bonding with my sister when playing it" (97). One *The Sims FreePlay* player discussed the way the game reminded her of her father, "because he got me and my brother into playing forever and a day ago, and he's not here anymore" (97). In a literature review that preceded her study, Sanders noted a lack of "substantial research regarding how the gaming experience and reading experience are similar" (45).

Sanders's study led to a subsequent book chapter, "Emotional Response to Gaming Producing Rosenblatt's Transaction" (2016). But this study was limited to one genre of game: massively multiplayer online games. Also, each of the games in Sanders's study is what is typically called a "AAA" game, a game produced or distributed by a major publisher and characterized by high-quality graphics, technical complexity, and a significant marketing budget. Whereas Sanders's research set out specifically to examine AAA or "mainstream" multiplayer games, our approach is more general and inclusive of mainstream, indie, art, serious, and experimental games.

A framework for applying Rosenblatt and reader-response theory to multimodalities in video games was also proposed in an article from digital literacies professor Sam von Gillern (2016): *Gamer Response and Decision (GRAD) Framework*. The GRAD Framework focuses on how "every individual has unique experiences, knowledge, skills, agency, self-efficacy, and goals, and [how] these components influence how people interpret and make decisions during video gameplay, which affects how the game unfolds as a unique experience for each gamer" (Von Gillern 2016, 665). Upton (2015) also cites Rosenblatt in his discussion of game aesthetics and narrative but does not dig deeply into the potential for a broader theory of player response in his initial work. We acknowledge and are building on this early research, as well as findings relevant from Dykehouse (2017) and Feldman (2018), who focused on reader-response theory and games in master's theses. Some of these articles are founded on media and literature professor John Alberti's (2008) essay connecting play in reading and gaming to media scholar John Fiske's (1987) idea of *active audiences* in TV spectatorship. Fiske (1987) observed how viewers were not merely passive spectators but rather transacted in ways similar to Rosenblatt's description of reader response.

Additionally, we acknowledge that there is a significant history of game analysis and criticism that borrows from other lenses of literary and media studies. Journals, such as *Game Studies* and *Games and Culture*, and the proceedings of conferences such as the Digital Games Research Association (DiGRA) have long published essays and articles that reflect the multifaceted backgrounds of many game scholars. Books on the analysis of games in the tradition of humanities and media studies include *Introduction to Game Analysis* (2019) by game studies professor Clara Fernández-Vara, whose background is in literature, film, and theater. There is also the book series Video Games and the Humanities, published by De Gruyter Oldenbourg, currently edited by Nathalie Aghoro, Iro Filippaki, Chris Kempshall, Esther MacCallum-Stewart, Jeremiah McCall, and Sascha Pöhlmann, which seeks to create a dialogue between literary studies, media studies, and game studies.

Our project here, however, is not to address how games might be part of the academic tradition of critical analysis but rather to open a discussion of how games are read by the broader audience of players. We do not delve into a particular lens or perspective, such as feminist, Marxist, or queer theory, in any direct sense—even as these may be found in the readings brought about by individual players. Rather, we hope to explore the *process* by which we can learn to become well-read players of our own *game experiences* and to go beyond the brief acknowledgment that players can have unique and personal experiences with games in the same manner as readers do with texts. Our destination is closer to Rosenblatt's belief, in line with Dewey's philosophy, that better readers make better citizens. The process of becoming a well-read player, like that of becoming a lifelong reader, involves not only the personal process of negotiating a text but also the social practice of developing and sharing ideas with others, and this practice, as we will see, can help us build the same skills we need to form more effective communities and participate in them more fully. When we explore the many ways in which games can be read aesthetically, as we do in the following chapters, we see that becoming a well-read player can give us insight into our own beliefs and prejudices—in situations in the game and in the world—and provoke us to reflect on these as we transform ourselves as players and as people.

2
Learning to Play Closely

It is an interesting problem that reading games aesthetically does not seem to be a natural extension of becoming a "better" game player. A reason for this may be the primarily efferent stance a player must take when learning to play a game. Whether it be reading and understanding the rules of a board game, grasping the controls of a video game, or even having a game explained to you by a friend, most gameplay situations begin with an efferent, informational stance as an entry point to the experience. Many players are even fearful or uncomfortable during these initial moments of a game, focused on knowing what to do first and what the goals of play are, and trying to get enough of a sense of the system to form their initial play strategy. So this efferent stance is completely understandable. We are introduced to a game with a strong need and desire to be in an information-gathering mode. And yet this information-gathering period is also where the most basic aesthetics of a game are introduced. The rules are written in the vocabulary of the game's objects, setting, and world. The game's mechanics and objectives are stated and taught to us in that same vocabulary. As described in chapter 1, we are not taught to click on images and animations in *Unpacking*—we are taught to open boxes. These images and animations represent familiar objects like boxes, toys, toothbrushes, and so on, and so even as we are learning the rules, grasping the information of what we need to understand and do, we are also learning the aesthetics of the game, its formal rules, its dramatic settings, its visual style, tone, challenges, as well as the kinds of complications we will face as a player.

As we move out of this necessary efferent stance, we can, if we are so inclined, take on a more aesthetic stance in our reading of the game. And sometimes we do; there are some games, like *Unpacking*, that *must* engage us aesthetically, or they will not engage us at all. We need only look at the many early reviews of so-called *walking simulators*, like *Gone Home* (Fullbright Games 2013), as we discuss in chapter 5, to see that if a game requires a primarily aesthetic stance in order to evoke engagement, there are many players who are unable or unwilling to move from the more efferent pleasures of gameplay (continual grasping of new features, mechanics, and challenge and skill-based interactions) to the more aesthetic pleasures of reading the game. Of course, there are aesthetic pleasures in the grasping of those mechanics and application of skills, but the ability to appreciate those formal aspects of games aesthetically is a part of this continuum between the efferent and aesthetic experience for players.

As we describe in chapter 1, the playing of a game is akin to the *event* of reading a text in transactional theory, or the game as experienced in Upton's situational theory. That event is created by the meeting of a text or a game with a unique player at a particular time in their life and situated in a certain context—*evoking* a reading, to use Rosenblatt's (1978) terminology. A young reader or player may experience a text very differently than an adult reader or player, evoking very different readings of the text.

When we are learning to read, we begin with phonics, vocabulary, and simple grammar, and then we move on to more complex stories with ideas and themes that are harder to parse. Similarly, with games, we generally begin with simple mechanics and activities, what game designers call the "verbs" of play, and as we become better players, we move on to games with more sophisticated systems. We may become better at abstracting possibilities out of complex strategic situations or responding more quickly to new information. But do we become better at recognizing and articulating the themes of a game, its relationship to our world, to the kinds of situations we are rehearsing within its boundaries? Do we begin to notice not only the "verbs" but also what we might call the "nouns," "adjectives," "adverbs," and increasingly complex metaphors and other more complex grammars of its play? Do we, without prompting or scaffolding, become better at evoking different or more complex readings of game texts? We argue that it is a lot to expect of players that they should grow their own aesthetics of games naturally, or naively, without prompting and scaffolding.

Some players clearly do become better at evoking an aesthetic response to games. In game designer Frank Lantz's (2023) *The Beauty of Games*, he describes his appreciation of *Serpentes* (Soulé 2015), an innovative variant of the classic action puzzle game *Snake*, where players must keep from colliding with objects in the game, including the snake itself, which gets harder to do as the snake grows longer. In *Serpentes*, objects in the game change their values from play to play. Lantz (2023) gushes about the experience of playing the game: "I love the way it feels in my brain. Every time I start a game of *Serpentes*, I have to deliberately flush out the registers of my short-term memory. This is a game in which forgetting is a key skill. . . . Like an exercise in homebrew neuroscience, the game shines a dim light into the normally invisible machinery of my brain" (3).

Lantz is clearly a high-level aesthetic player, someone who has for many years trained himself not only to play games *well* but to play games *aesthetically*—that is, to notice and articulate the micro aspects of his own aesthetic experience with games. There are others, of course, like those writers and theorists mentioned in the precedents in chapter 1, who have applied the ideas of literary and media studies to gameplay. The curators of the web journal *Critical Distance* have for many years archived some of the best discussions around games under a mission statement to answer the perennial question, "Where is all the good writing about games?" (Critical Distance 2023). Similarly, other web journals such as *Unwinnable, Videodame,* and *Bullet Points Monthly* curate criticism, personal essays, poetry, and artwork inspired by game readings. One interesting recent publication is *Critical Hits: Writers Playing Video Games* (Lennon and Machado 2023), a compilation of personal essays about gameplay that, perhaps because of the authors' experiences responding to written texts, explore the kind of personal readings that escape many more traditional game players and writers. But even well-intentioned game writing, such as Carnegie Mellon University's Entertainment Technology Center (ETC) Well Played book series, which we discuss at length in the following chapter, often falls into an efferent emphasis on walkthroughs of features or levels. And, of course, game journalism and reviews are, almost without exception, focused on the technological advances and efferent offerings of games. It is a rare exception that we find a journalist or writer like Brendan Keogh, whose critical reading of *Spec Ops: The Line* (Yager 2012), which we discuss in chapter 3, or Tom Bissell, whose discussion of his play of *Fallout 3* (Bethesda 2008) during the 2008 elections is certainly a form of aesthetic reading. So where are all the other aesthetic players? Where can we find the multitude of brilliant and beautiful discussions of play from players across all backgrounds and cultures? Discussions that can inspire us in our own experiences with games? For the most part, and in the experience of the broader range of players, they are not to be found or at least acknowledged. And much of this has to do with the culture around what games are, who plays them, how we talk about that play, and what skills we need to fully appreciate them.

We propose that aesthetic play is a set of metacognitive skills that we should be training players, young and old, to practice. It is a type of literacy that is deeply related to the way in which we learn to appreciate other art forms, such as literature, painting, film, and music. We cannot expect every player to naturally and naively become an aesthetic reader of their own play without understanding the steps they can take to practice this type of literacy. The following chapters outline ways of approaching games thoughtfully that will change our expectations of what we are meant to take away from playful experiences and make us better at appreciating the nuances of our own gameplay to read those experiences for the aesthetic events they are. Our goal is to learn to play games with an eye to what is going on in our thoughts and emotions while we play. It is a different way of playing, much like we take on a different way of seeing when we learn to appreciate painting or other visual arts or a different way of listening when we learn to appreciate music. We are still enjoying the primary experience, the visual or aural beauty, but we are also seeing the patterns that make up that beauty, the spill of light, the crescendo of horns, or in a game, the moment when a move or mechanic expresses something meaningful about the world that changes the way we will see it ever after.

Learning to Read Literature, Learning to Read Games

In our quest to understand these skills, it is illuminating to look at the ways in which literature—specifically children's literature—teaches young readers to move from a more simplistic, efferent reading style to a more complex, aesthetic style of reading. Children's literature teaches how to move beyond basic literacy skills, like phonics and introductory grammar, to read for meaning, identification, emotional growth, and aesthetic appreciation. The learning curve of appreciating children's literature is an important process for young readers, as it helps build skills for them to appreciate more complex and challenging literature as they grow.

In the influential article "Text as Teacher: The Beginning of *Charlotte's Web*" (1985), Perry Nodelman examines how E. B. White's book *Charlotte's Web* (1952) teaches children how to aesthetically engage with literature by including a kind of tutorial in its first two chapters. Nodelman describes the way in which readers, including children, approach each new experience with an existing cognitive map. When a story or reading experience differs from our existing cognitive map, it causes us to notice those differences, adapt, and compose a new cognitive map encompassing more complex explanations. In this way, as children begin by being read fairy tales and other short stories, they form simple cognitive maps about how stories work. As Nodelman writes, the first two chapters of *Charlotte's Web* conform to this kind of simple storytelling while also providing an entry point to a story that will eventually explore more complex ideas about friendship, loyalty, death, and grief.

Charlotte's Web begins when Fern, a farmer's daughter, begs her father to spare the life of a runt pig, feeling that it is unjust that he should die simply because he was born too small. Fern saves Wilbur's life and then plays at being his mother. She feeds him milk with a bottle, takes him for walks in a stroller, and puts him tenderly to bed in a box by the stove. An adult reading these two chapters will recognize hints at the larger conflict to come, in the smell of bacon cooking in the kitchen and the attitude of Fern's parents about the little pig's place in their world. But, for a child, these first two chapters are a comfortable and simple story about a girl caring for her pet pig, a familiar entry point following a known cognitive map, as Nodleman (1985) argues, that allows "young readers who know only simple fiction" to become ready to respond to the more complex story that follows (115). These first two chapters of *Charlotte's Web* form a kind of bridge from the fairy tale world of a girl caring for her cute little pig to the rest of the book, which will bring us into a world far more complex than playing at motherhood.

What Nodelman (1985) calls the "fairy tale" of the first two chapters ends when Wilbur becomes old enough and large enough to live in a barn (110). At this point, the story and the storytelling change. Now, rather than a simple tale about a girl saving a pig, we find ourselves in a world of talking animals—a microcosm of society where Wilbur is the naive young hero learning about life from a wily rat, a busybody goose, and a "bloodthirsty" spider who turns out to be not only wise and kind but a loyal friend (White 1952, 39). The storytelling shifts from the basic naturalism of Fern's world to a kind of poetic description of the sense-focused world of the animals. From Wilbur's perspective, "The barn was very large. It was very old. It smelled of hay and it smelled of manure. It smelled of the perspiration of tired horses and the wonderful sweet breath of patient cows. It often had a sort of peaceful smell—as though nothing bad could ever happen again in the world. It smelled of grain and of harness dressing and of axle grease and of rubber boots and of new rope" (White 1952, 13). As Nodelman (1985) writes, "Not only does this passage set the scene for the rest of the novel; it also introduces its central images, its central structural patterns, and its central themes" (116). The basic structural pattern of *Charlotte's Web*, as per Nodelman, is the list: lists that suggest the "glorious multitudinousness" of life and the "glorious variety of everything" (116). These lists are filled with beautiful new vocabulary for young readers—descriptive nouns and adjectives that build a world that feels naturalistic and real because of their appeal to the senses so that, though we are reading a story about talking animals, we are evoking a world that has stronger sense ties to the natural world than the simplistic fairy tale world of the first two chapters.

When young readers enjoy *Charlotte's Web*, they are led through the gateway of the first two chapters: a brief moral tale about a girl who saves a pig from being killed and turns him into her pretend child. This kind of pretend play is easily mapped to their existing understanding of both stories and pets. It is a safe and simple fairy tale story where justice is simple and easily prevails. The following narrative, once Wilbur goes to live in the barn, shows us a more complex society, where justice is a more difficult concept and death is a real possibility for our naive hero. This bulk of the story forms a more sophisticated text that uses the literary structure of lengthy descriptive lists to evoke its very detailed and immersive world. In this world, Wilbur's life is in danger again, and this time is not saved so easily. Fern, who saved his life as a baby and played mother to him, now recedes into the background of the story, sitting on an old milking stool, watching and listening to the animals. Even though she can understand their conversations, she never engages in them and never takes another action in the entire novel to help or interfere with Wilbur's safety. Rather, it is Charlotte, a large, gray spider, who takes Fern's place in the story as a more mature motherly figure. Charlotte's relationship with Wilbur goes beyond babying him; she patiently teaches him about their world while still keeping from him the reality of its most difficult lessons. Wilbur trusts her like a true friend or mother who promises to save him, even if it means putting her own life at risk.

In *The Act of Reading: A Theory of Aesthetic Response* (1978), literary scholar Wolfgang Iser describes the way in which sophisticated texts do not adhere to our existing cognitive maps but rather exert a *modifying influence* on the reader that forces us to reconsider our existing ideas. As children read past the first two chapters of *Charlotte's Web*, they encounter a new kind of world: one where they are challenged to transfer their attention from Fern to Wilbur, as our main character, and then from Fern to Charlotte, as the other motherly figure. In doing so, we are led into a narrative where we begin to worry about Wilbur's potential death as if he were a human character. No longer pretending that he is a pet or a baby, we are fully involved with Wilbur, his world, and his fate as we, and young readers, will eventually learn to be involved in the human condition. It is a set of literary stepping stones, a tutorial from fairy tale stories with easy endings to a more complex experience, using rich descriptive language to bring alive characters and a world that is not fair or just but requires struggle and friendship to live in. As Nodelman (1985) concludes, "In telling his story twice, once from the viewpoint of innocence and in terms of naive literary skills, and then from the viewpoint of experience and in terms of sophisticated literary skills, White gives young readers the experience they need to transcend their own innocence as readers" (126). He also points out that this two-part structure can be found in many other children's novels, including A. A. Milne's (1926) *Pooh* books, *The Wind in the Willows* (Grahame 1908), *Treasure Island* (Stevenson 188), *Anne of Green Gables* (Montgomery 1908), and *Harriet the Spy* (Fitzhugh 1964) to name just a few. All these texts use this established pattern of a two-part story to act as teachers of narrative competencies.

Are there parallels to these kinds of literary stepping stones in games? Is there an as-yet unacknowledged way of leading players from the simple state of learning how to play a game to reading the experience of playing the game in a more sophisticated and aesthetic way? We know that there are some players who are simply more attuned to their experiences in this way—we have seen examples from sensitive and articulate players like Lantz, as well as the students and colleagues we quote in chapter 7, of aesthetic readings that suggest that there are, indeed, many players who learn to read games aesthetically. And as authors of this book, we have practiced this kind of reading ourselves, which is why we are so interested in seeing this type of reading more recognized and practiced. Game designers like Upton and Fullerton have written about these kinds of experiences in design texts such as *Situational Game Design* (Upton 2018) and *Game Design Workshop* (2004, 2024). And we know that there are many other players who naturally find deep and meaningful expressions in their play. And yet the practice of reading and articulating our lived-through play experiences closely is not typically discussed and rarely considered a core skill in media, literature, or game studies classrooms. The general expectation of thinking about and critiquing games is that of the review, a kind of analytical writing that focuses on discussing the success or failure of features, graphics, and gameplay; not of articulating the lived-through, aesthetic experience of players.

What makes some players able to notice their aesthetic experiences in games so distinctly and to articulate ideas about that lived experience so clearly? To answer this question, we can look at the tradition of "close reading" in literature for a model. As we've already seen, children's literature is often structured in ways that build on earlier narrative competencies to introduce more sophisticated experiences. Additionally, children are taught, beginning as early as kindergarten, to read texts "closely"—that is, to analyze and interpret the writing for figurative language, metaphors, motifs, imagery, symbolism, and other literary devices. In *Charlotte's Web*, for example, the device of foreshadowing is used in the very first scene of the story. As Fern asks her mother where her father is going with the axe, breakfast is cooking, and the smell of bacon fills the kitchen. This foreshadows Wilbur's potential fate and the danger of being fattened and killed that he experiences throughout the story. Later, in the microcosm of society that is the farm, metaphor is used to build a sense of that natural community. For example, "The crickets felt it was their duty to warn everybody that summertime cannot last forever. Even on the most beautiful days in the whole year—the days when summer is changing into fall—the crickets spread the rumor of sadness and change" (White 1952, 113). The lovely metaphor compares the sounds made by the crickets to the spread of rumor and gossip by busybodies in society.

Learning to read closely leads readers to gain a new kind of knowledge about their own experiences with texts. The stages of close reading lead students from *what* (being able to retell the literal meaning of a story or text) to *how* (looking at word choice, syntax, point of view, and perspective) to *why* (thinking about the author's intent, credibility, and making connections to the world outside the text including our own experience with the text). This kind of close observation and interpretation of not only *what* a text is telling us but *how* a text tells its story—and how that telling makes us *feel* about that story—is a key component of close reading. Although many literature teachers do tend to focus on close reading as a method of assessment—asking students to provide textual evidence in the form of examples of these literary devices—close reading is, in fact, a subjective process. This may be seen as a limitation, or as a springboard, depending on the teacher's or the reader's goals. In literacy classrooms, close readers are taught to underline, use sticky notes, and annotate in the margins. They are taught to evoke a reading, what Rosenblatt would call a "poem" or a "lived-through response," as part of the close reading process and to capture that reading simultaneously with their experience. This is a moment where the dichotomy between efferent and aesthetic readings coalesces as we participate in an intertwined process of meaning-making, awareness, and the capturing of our reading. After this close reading occurs, students are then taught to look for literary patterns and devices and for breaks in those patterns from which they can form an interpretation and a personal response. This is an iterative, looping process, from observation to interpretation to response, and back again.

Where do we see this kind of layered close reading process in games? Quite clearly, we see a version of it in the tutorial levels of essentially every game, which must teach not only how to use and manipulate a game's mechanics and controls, but also to understand those mechanics and controls within the context of the game world. When we pick up the controller to play a video game, we bring to it the same kind of cognitive map that Nodelman discusses in terms of children's narrative. Our expectations are built first upon our experiences in the world, and later, upon our experiences with other games. For example, Fullerton can recall viscerally her first experience playing *Super Mario Bros.* (Nintendo 1985). It was not her first video game, but it was a magical—and instructional—experience:

> I remember learning to run and jump and bump my head up against the blocks. The music was so joyful and the colors so bright and captivating. My siblings and I would pass the controller around and play for hours. It was summertime and our parents told us to go outside, but we were living in a magical world of mushrooms and Goombas. We were learning a whole new language of play, and every level was a new set of vocabulary words, new things you could do. Our brains were on fire with new knowledge.

Platforming games have become a staple of game experiences. Their central mechanics—running, jumping, evading and destroying enemies, power-ups, moving platforms, lock and keys, and more—form the basis of this popular genre of play. The vocabulary of platformers is filled with verbs like "run," "jump," "bump," "pick up," and so on. As with all genres of play, these kinds of mechanics, in combination, create a familiar foundation for players and allow for the development of an expertise—or a familiar cognitive map. As players, in the same way that readers build vocabularies of words, we learn vocabularies of play. Being familiar with a mechanic, for example, opens possibilities of noticing differences in that mechanic from game to game and expanding our *understanding* of it. So, "running" in *Super Mario Bros.* has a feeling to it: a loopy, silly playtime feeling. Running in *Sonic the Hedgehog* (Sega 1991) is different. It is fast and aggressive—not aggressive in a mean way, but rather, in a rush, rush, rush, speedster way. It is exciting to play *Sonic* in a way that *Mario* is not. *Mario* is fun, of course, but *Sonic* gets your heartbeat racing. And if you stop running, Sonic, the impatient little guy, crosses his arms, taps his fingers at you as if to say, "Get going! What's the holdup?!" It evokes an entirely different experience.

In *Persuasive Games: The Expressive Power of Video Games* (2007), Ian Bogost argues that players create meaning by identifying the gaps between real-world systems and their abstracted versions in video games. We see this in the aesthetic reading of *Unpacking* in chapter 1 when Fullerton is surprised by the inability to leave the character's toys out on the floor. The gap between her understanding of the real-world experience of a child's room (with the most-used toys scattered on the floor) and *Unpacking*'s unstated requirement that all toys be put away neatly created a potential for her to fill in this gap with her own understanding of the system—an imaginary parent who enforced that rule. *Narrative gaps* are a key concept in reader-response theory as well, creating opportunities for readers to engage their imagination in the interpretation process. As readers, we each bring with us our own experiences and understandings and use these to anticipate what might happen and to fill in gaps in narratives as well as in systems. These gaps may be as simple as a cut from an open-ended scene where a character has a decision to make to a later moment in the story, leaving a reader uncertain about what choice has been made, to a much larger ellipses of time, sometimes years, opening the opportunity for readers to use their imagination to understand what has occurred in the intervening time. These ellipses may occur between scenes in a novel, episodes in a TV show, films in an ongoing franchise, or multiple games set in a single world. Media scholar Henry Jenkins has referred to these types of gaps or *ellipses* as a formal aspect of *transmedia storytelling,* in which story worlds and characters are developed over time and across media in ways that purposefully invite readers, viewers, and players to engage their imaginations in extending and exploring the story world (Jenkins 2006). To use another example from *Unpacking,* we know that between each level, as we unpack the character's belongings yet again, much has happened that we have not seen. But we fill in the gaps of those experiences based on the items we unpack and the new living situation we find ourselves in. For example, in the scene that comes after the "boyfriend level" that Fullerton describes, we find the character moving back into her childhood bedroom—the same one we unpacked in the very first level. We can fill in the gaps of the narrative with our own experiences from failed relationships and having taken step backs in our development to regroup, go home, grow, and get ready to try again.

Similar to the way that Iser (1978) argues that a more sophisticated narrative text exerts an influence on us and forces us to reconsider our existing cognitive map of a narrative situation, the abstracted situation of a video game, when compared with our understanding of either its real-world counterpart or another video game's similar but different abstraction, causes us to reconsider its meaning. So "running" in *Mario* means the kind of silly skipping running we might do across a field of flowers, whereas "running" in *Sonic* means a kind of manic relay race across hot lava and spikes. In essence, we are "doing" the same thing: pushing a controller button or joystick to the right. However, in the vocabulary of play, we are discovering that there can be adverbs, and even adjectives, of play, as well as verbs. As we've already discussed, game designers often describe the activities of play as the "verbs" of the game system. What can a player do in the game? Can they run, jump, or climb? Can they collect, craft, or trade? Can they cast a magic spell or speak to another character? All these activities are recognizable verbs that game players become familiar with as they learn to play simple games and then, later, more complex games that may use the same vocabulary of verbs. But what about the "adverbs" and "adjectives" of play? *How* are we running? Quickly? Carelessly? For our lives? Long distance or short sprints? Do we tire? Do we run until we begin to fly? Why are we running at all? To read games closely, we must pay attention to these aspects of their vocabulary as well.

In recent years, a popular genre of play has become something called the "narrative platformer." The idea of a narrative platformer is that as we move our character through the world, we experience a story that may be environmental—that is, discovered in bits of story embedded in the world that may be cued by meeting other characters that we can talk to or interact with—or the story may emerge from interacting with the kind of descriptive game mechanics discussed above. These narrative platformers include games like *Braid* (Number None 2008), where you play as Tim, a man searching for a princess who has ostensibly been snatched by a horrible and evil monster. The game uses traditional platforming verbs but also introduces a set of time-based puzzle mechanics that not only complicate the platforming but also intertwine with both of these sets of verbs to complicate the telling of the story itself. As with the example of *Charlotte's Web*, we are told the story of *Braid* twice: once in a simplistic, fairy tale fashion in which our character, Tim, plays the hero in search of a princess, just like in *Super Mario Bros*. We run and jump and puzzle our way through the levels to reach our princess. But as we get closer to her, the time-rewinding mechanics begin to show us a more complex story. When Fullerton played, she journaled:

> I realize that I, playing as Tim, am the monster from whom the princess is running. All my progress in the game has brought me to this surprising moment of self-awareness that twists all of my assumptions about the platforming mechanics, games, heroes, goodness, princesses, desire, and fairy tales. My understanding of the game must be replaced with a deeper interpretation of all the verbs and mechanics of its story, and, as I see it now run backward in time, every positive adverb or adjective I had associated with what I thought was heroic gameplay is replaced with a predatory one. I am filled with regret and a sense of lost innocence. The simple verbs of my happy-go-lucky, childish platforming gameplay will never be the same.

Not every player has had this particular epiphany, of course, and not every player will have it with *Braid* or within a platforming game (see figure 2.1). But this epiphany, this shift in understanding of how rich a gameplay experience can be, is the shift from playing efferently to playing closely and aesthetically. When we play efferently, we learn how to jump on a platform. But when we play closely, we think about what kind of a jump it is. A playful jump? A desperate jump? A bounding jump? And the platform? Is it a familiar

Figure 2.1
Platforming in *Braid*.

one? One that we've seen before and know leads us to safety? Or is it one that leads to adventure? Can we see where it leads, or are we jumping into space with an unknown destination? Or the princess? Is she the naive helpless princess of a fairy tale? Or is she an empowered woman using every mechanic available to her to escape the unwanted attention of an ex-lover? What does our jump mean, both mechanically and narratively? This core competency of observing and noticing our own play—a type of game literacy—is directly related to the way we learn to observe and notice our lived experience with a written text. The text in a game is multimodal, of course, and includes cues from aural, visual, narrative, and interactive elements, but it is a text nonetheless, and our play within that text can be read closely and understood as a lived experience that provokes an aesthetic response that will be as deep as we are ready and willing to have with it.

There is a wonderful double meaning in the term *scaffolding*, attributed to psychologist Jerome Bruner in the 1960s. Bruner was building on psychologist Lev Vygotsky's (1978) concept of the *zone of proximal development,* "the distance between the [child's] actual development level as determined by independent problem solving and the level of potential development as determined through problem solving under adult guidance or in collaboration with more capable peers" (86). Bruner, and many educators, use the term *scaffolding* to describe the way that learners are guided to grasp and master new concepts with guidance from the more capable peer. Like a building under construction, scaffolding helps support learners from one stage of understanding to the next. Game designers have adopted this term as well, describing the way that tutorials and early game levels teach players the rules and objectives of the game step by step, level by level.

In Bruner's (1966) theory of development, he describes learning as a three-stage process scaffolded by teachers, in much the same way that games scaffold their experiences for players. The first stage is experiential learning, or what Bruner (1966) calls *enactive representation.* If we take the example of our platforming games, this first stage of learning would be the hands-on action of manipulating our character across the screen. Pressing buttons and seeing that the character jumps, perhaps hearing a cheery musical sound each time we jump successfully. Players learn that by pressing buttons and moving a joystick, we can do things in the game that we recognize from real life. The next stage, when our memories become linked to experiences, is *iconic representation* (Bruner 1966). We have an iconic concept of a "jump" in a game that we understand and that we've mapped to our real-world experience of a "jump." No matter that one is physical and the other is virtual, in the same way that we recognize the word "jump" in a book and map that word to a real-world jump, so, too, can we understand a game jump to represent a jump. This leads to what Bruner (1966) calls *symbolic representation,* where we apply what we've learned in a way that shows we have mastered the concept. In a game, this may mean using a jump in a new and more complex way that helps us master a difficult level. Or, if we are reading our play more closely, it may also mean thinking about how we have jumped and what it means. It may mean that we have mastered not only the activity of jumping but also the reading of that activity as a symbolic event. In our example of the platformer, a jump is not really a jump until a player has "read" it as such, and if they have read it closely, it may mean more than just a jump.

To give an example of a game that does a good job of supporting players to move from efferent to close play, in much the same way that *Charlotte's Web* provides an entry point for young readers to move from efferent to close reading, we can look at *Lost Words: Beyond the Page* (Sketchbook Games 2021), a narrative platform game about a young girl, Izzy, who aspires to be a writer. *Lost Words* uses the same basic platforming verbs already described in *Super Mario Bros.* and *Braid*. In the opening level of *Lost Words*, we learn the basic verbs of the game. It's a platformer, so there's running and jumping, of course. But in this first level, the quirk of the game is revealed: we are running and jumping on the words of a young girl's journal. Izzy's grandmother knows that she dreams of being a writer, and so gives her a journal for her birthday. As Izzy writes, we play as a tiny version of her, navigating the words on the page, sometimes moving them around, sometimes using them to scrub the page and reveal images, and sometimes jumping across what seem to be impossible distances between words to find our way to the little door torn in each page that transitions us to the next layout (see figure 2.2). "A writer writes," Izzy's grandmother tells her, and so this first level also introduces us to the other half of this game: Estoria.

Estoria is Izzy's storyland. We help her write by choosing words in the journal: a name for the character, a color for her robe, and an adjective that describes her personality. Interestingly, as we choose these words, the journal itself teaches us to read them closely. Each reveal of a potential character name, for example, also reveals a note from Izzy about the kind of character that might suit that name. Grace "sounds noble, or spiritual maybe? Georgia seems

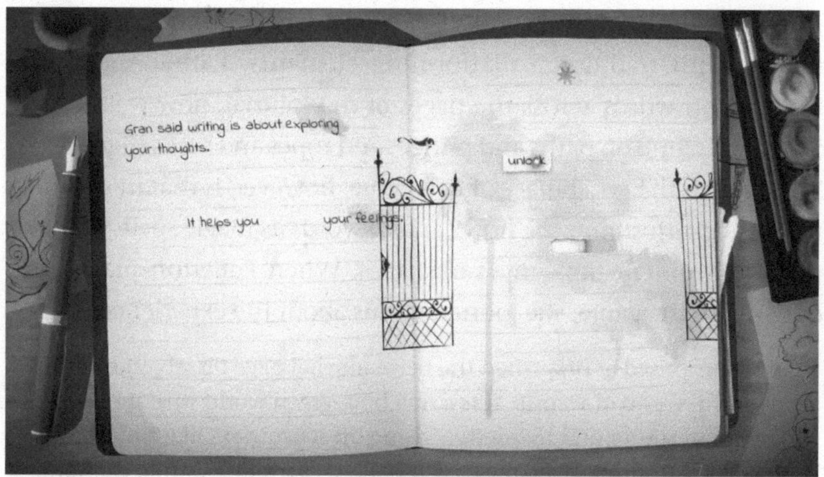

Figure 2.2
Platforming in *Lost Words*'s journal.

like "someone who confronts monsters!" Robyn sounds "free like a bird in the sky." The choices we make to define the main character of Izzy's story will change some of the dialogue and objects in the game but not the overall narrative arc. The adventure that happens in Estoria is affected not by our choice of character name or attributes but by Izzy's experiences in the frame narrative of her life at home as well as by our ability to read closely the relationship between these two narratives. Like *Charlotte's Web*, and like many other examples of children's literature, *Lost Words* tells its story twice, and in doing so, helps us to move from efferent to close reading of those intertwined stories. When we begin the game, we may think we are simply platforming on words as a clever visual design. But after the early levels, we begin to realize the depth of meaning being created by these intertwined experiences. In the journal levels, we play as a miniature Izzy, running and jumping as she writes about her life experiences. In Estoria, we play as Grace, Georgia, or Robyn (whichever name we have chosen) as she learns to become a thoughtful and resourceful "Guardian" of her home village.

The scenes in Estoria are visualized in beautifully painted 2D images with traditional platforming elements. Rather than platforming on words across the pages of the journal, now we run and jump and climb on paths and bridges and ropes and rocks (figure 2.3). The twist in the vocabulary of this game, however, is that in addition to classic platforming; we now can use words as magic spells to make our way through the game's obstacles. When Fullerton played the opening of the game, she journaled this about the experience:

> I am surprised at first when the beige journal page dissolves into the colorful world of Estoria. It is a rich blue-green world with motes flying in the air and tiny letters rising off what looks like a magic platform in front of a large tree. Izzy keeps speaking to me, though, keeping continuity with her journal, so I realize that she is the narrator of both stories, giving me a familiar perspective. Now, rather than telling me about herself, however, she is telling me about the character I've chosen—Grace, in my case, who is wearing a purple robe and is curious, compassionate, and smart. As I move Grace along in the world, there are two kinds of text on the screen, and I'm immediately curious about this. There is dialogue, like when

Figure 2.3
Platforming in Estoria, Izzy's storyland in *Lost Words*.

> Grace greets a firefly, and there is descriptive text talking about how the firefly floated down and began to buzz around Grace. I feel like I'm in a picture book, and when it's time to get up and run home along the hills and bridges, that descriptive text of this book has come to vibrant life for me to interact with.

The journey through Estoria, which begins as a simple fantasy story, changes after the first level of the game. Once we have learned the basic platforming mechanics of both the journal and Estoria, and we have used our first magic word, "Rise," to overcome some simple platforming mechanics, we return to the journal for some bad and unexpected news: Izzy's grandmother has had a stroke and is in the hospital. Izzy is shocked and upset, and the shock of this experience is reflected by a sudden tragedy in her story. We return to the peaceful land of Estoria to find it in flames, the village destroyed. Now we are given magic words like "Repair" and "Extinguish" to fight our way to the firefly shrine that has protected the village, only to find it destroyed and the fireflies gone. Like Izzy's real world, the world of Estoria is in chaos. The adventure follows the stages of Izzy's grief: shock, denial, anger, bargaining, guilt, depression, and finally, acceptance. When Fullerton played, she wrote about the grief that Izzy/Grace face in the intertwined stories:

> When Izzy finds out that her grandmother has had a stroke, the words I am platforming on literally turn upside down, dumping my character down off the pages as she says, "I have a weird feeling in my stomach." I know that feeling and I'm suddenly in a state of anxiety about what is about to happen. Izzy says, "I don't want to believe it. I can't lose her." I jump across the words, but they shatter, and I fall again into a deep, deep black. When I come back, it is to Estoria, and I know that Izzy's pain has sent her here to write, to figure out how to deal with this moment. I have to figure it out too, and I'm dreading what will happen next.

Each of the levels and challenges that the player faces along the journey is related to challenges that Izzy is going through in her own young life. She is literally writing what she knows, and we are facing the metaphoric versions of her emotional conflicts. When she faces a fiery giantess full of anger, (see figure 2.4) her compassion allows her to move past her fear, and the giant rage monster transforms into a small flame named "Lump," who becomes a friend and comes with her on the next phase of her journey. Fullerton shares her experiences in this moment:

> The giant fire woman slams the ground and screams about how alone she is, how filled with rage she is. It's scary. The scariest moment in the game so far. But the fire woman doesn't push the moment—not yet. She leaves us with a warning. As we rest for a moment, Grace wonders about what has made the fire woman so angry, and as that happens, I'm able to add the word "burn" to my spell book. Then, I can choose why I think the firewoman is angry. Is she alone? Unappreciated? Or Misunderstood? I choose "Misunderstood." Grace muses on my choice. "She smashes stuff because no one understands her. I get that." Izzy narrates: "Grace vowed to be more understanding if they met again." Now, as I use my new word to move forward, clearing the way by burning debris out of my path, Izzy tells me that the resolution to be more understanding has made a difference for Grace. "A heaviness lifted from her heart." I'm happy for Grace, and I know that Izzy, by writing this story, is feeling the same release of her anger. This learning serves all three of us

Figure 2.4
Izzy faces the fire giantess in *Lost Words*.

> well when we meet the giant firewoman again. Screaming in rage, she chases us across burning platforms. During an exchange filled with anger, Grace realizes that there might be a better approach, telling the rage-filled giantess, "When I'm angry, I take a few deep breaths." This changes the entire battle. Suddenly, my rage-filled foe transforms into a tiny lump of flames. Her voice is now cute, like a child's, and we introduce ourselves to one another. I'm relieved, charmed, and I understand and feel connected to the lesson here.

The emotions that Grace is learning about in Estoria are directly related to those that Izzy is facing in her real life. And as we learn that her grandmother is not getting better, and is sadly fading away in the hospital, the lessons become more and more difficult. As Izzy faces the varying stages of her grief, she transforms them through her journal into her creative writing, and as we play, we help her overcome them in both versions of the story.

As in *Charlotte's Web*, *Lost Words* uses two versions of its story to scaffold players into concern for a character who is dealing with difficult emotions and to connect gameplay, specifically the "verbs" of platforming, to a more sophisticated vocabulary of play. This new vocabulary of gameplay uses words themselves as the basis of game mechanics that prompt us to explore grief, growth, and what it means to "read" our experiences of play. Interestingly, the writer of *Lost Words*, Rhianna Pratchett, is the daughter of fantasy novelist Terry Pratchett, which may account for the game's strong literary sensibility. Like *Charlotte's Web*, it teaches us that it is all right to feel strong, complicated emotions about the things that are happening in our lives, and it also offers a model for dealing with those emotions through journaling and creative writing. As we play *Lost Words*, we learn not just to solve the game's puzzles using the two different forms of word-based mechanics but also to *read* how the game's puzzles and problems relate to Izzy's turbulent emotional journey. And we are rewarded for playing the game with active, engaged emotions. If we were to play *Lost Words* without opening our full emotional selves to the process of understanding its mechanics and story, we would miss most of the meaning of the game. When we realize that our compassion for Lump can minimize the power of her anger, and make the same connection for Izzy's anger about her grandmother's declining health, we are then prepared to make the same connection to our own lives. Even as an adult, playing *Lost Words* has a kind of revelatory feel to it, as can be seen in Fullerton's journal entries.

As with *Charlotte's Web,* what we discover and connect to in our play of *Lost Words* will depend on our readiness to "read" this experience at a deeper level than just being able to perform its platforming activities. Simply enacting the verbs of its play will not result in a full reading of *Lost Words*. We will also need to bring an ability to connect that gameplay with how it makes us feel and to observe and notice those feelings. Just as *Charlotte's Web* leads us to have empathy for all creatures great and small, runt pig or bloodthirsty spider, and to care about justice for each of them, *Lost Words* leads us to recognize the importance of articulating our feelings, accepting them, and creatively turning them into the narratives of our lives. Each of these experiences—novel and game—scaffolds us step by step from fear to compassion, indifference to caring, and gives us, as players, greater and greater permission to explore our emotions around our characters, situations, and challenges. We begin by observing and connecting, by reading and playing closely, for meaning and emotional response, and we grow into a different way of playing.

3 Reading a Game Deeply

In Frank Lantz's (2023) *The Beauty of Games,* he discusses the concept of *deep play,* which he equates to composer Pauline Oliveros's concept of *deep listening* in music. Lantz and Oliveros both describe the practice of "active, focused attention" on one's personal experience with a game or with music. "What might we discover if we applied the same technique to our experience of games?" Lantz asks (37). As an experienced designer and player of games trained in art history, Lantz's own answers to that question are quite different from most players. He is already open and attentive to his own internal process, able to articulate his answers clearly and beautifully, making connections to his life, to other media, and to the wider aesthetic realm of games.

When we play deeply, we take on an aesthetic stance and we are free to explore our own thoughts and feelings about experiences in games. We must be open to active exploration of our own emotions. This means we must be present in the moment-to-moment playing of the game and also be able to notice and articulate our own internal "feelingscape." Being able to notice our own feelings about an experience and articulate them to ourselves is a difficult thing to do. This is why teachers scaffold children's literature so carefully to help young readers learn how to recognize and articulate how a story is making them feel. We can think about the same process with games. As we begin to read games, it helps to start with games that allow us to feel safe, confident, included, and welcome to explore our emotional responses. For example, many players who are not traditional game players feel welcome to play so-called walking simulators like *Gone Home* even though these games may be scoffed at by more traditional gamers. In *Gone Home,* the player takes on the role of Katie Greenbriar, a young woman returning home after an extended trip to Europe. The game takes place on a dark and stormy night, and no one is home to welcome Katie back. We search the Greenbrier house, trying to figure out what has happened, finding pieces of narrative in audio journals from Katie's younger sister Sam strewn around the house along with other clues to the story. Journalist Emily Morganti (2013) writes on *Adventure Gamers,* "Some players want action—there are games out there for you. Others want puzzles, and you have plenty of options, too. Me, I crave games that suck me into a story I can care about, introduce me to characters I can empathize with, transport me to a world I don't want to leave" (para. 14). A walking simulator, as Morganti suggests, is a game in which the interactions are focused on exploration and discovery of narrative elements rather than what might be thought of as more directly active verbs of play such as combat or solving puzzles. When Morganti writes about her experiences in *Gone Home,* she doesn't go so far as to give us her personal reading of the game, but she does touch on what makes this kind of game inviting for our discussion of deep play. "Most of what you do is 'optional,'" she writes, "meaning you could finish the game without it, but these optional discoveries have a cumulative effect and the designers have done such a good job of making you care about the characters that you'll want to keep looking. Interestingly, as I got closer to the big reveal at the end, I became even more meticulous and thorough in my exploration. The more I knew, the more

I wanted to know" (Morganti 2013, para. 5). When Fullerton played *Gone Home*, she journaled:

> I see a door at the end of the hall with a radioactive warning poster on it. This must be Sam's room. I poke around the room and find typical teenage stuff. She likes riot grrrl bands. It's not until I get to the bathroom that my heart skips a beat. There is blood in the tub (figure 3.1). I flip the lights on, and no, it's not blood, but red hair dye! I realize that Sam has dyed her hair—maybe not the horror I expected, but given what I've learned about her family, probably not with her parents' approval. I bet this caused a problem. As I pick up the bottle of red dye from the linoleum floor, I hear Sam's voice telling me about the experience, but again, it's not what I expected. It turns out it was Lonnie's hair dye. Sam was just helping her dye her roots. She talks about how intimate it is to touch someone else's scalp. As she tells the story, I poke around the bathroom cabinets, looking at her tampons and hairbrush. I'm so nosy. That feels intimate too. I'm lurking in this relationship when Sam tells me that as she and Lonnie looked in the mirror together, Lonnie surprised her by saying "You're so beautiful." It's a very touching moment, and I realize that

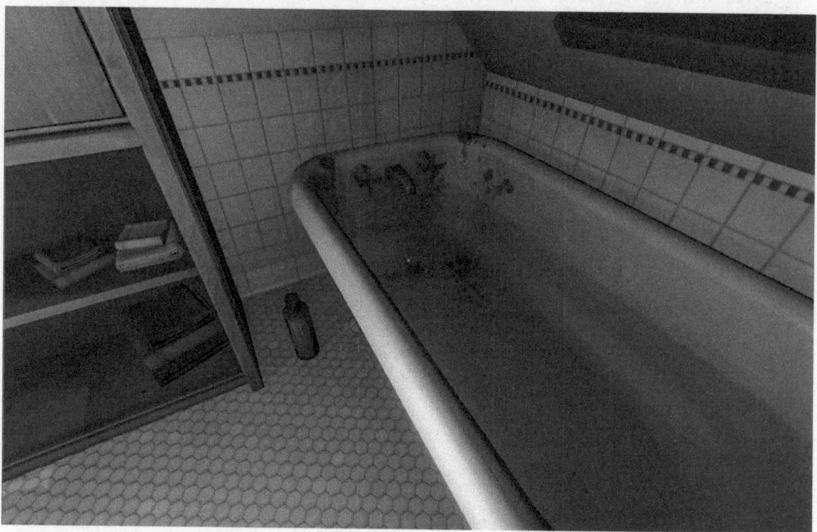

Figure 3.1
Gone Home: finding blood in the tub?

> this revelation is what Sam's 1990s parents are going to react to, not the red hair dye. This relationship just took a giant step toward the conflict I've been sensing since I opened the front door of the house.

Some players clearly do become better at evoking an aesthetic response to games. They are able to read their play closely, notice their responses and emotions, and create interpretations of those responses in the same way that they might form an interpretation of a piece of literature, a film, a painting, or a theater performance. These are not necessarily players who are "better" at the game than others or who win more often, but they are players who are playing deeply in the game while also noticing how they are feeling and thinking while they are playing. Perhaps the earliest recorded example of the deep play of a video game is David Sudnow's personal recollection of his fascination with *Breakout* (Atari 1972). In the book *Pilgrim in the Microworld* (1983), Sudnow writes,

> Playing *Breakout* again and again and again, through the slow phase and fast, from the one to the other to the other, I hit slam after slam after slam after slam, and was nodding, and bobbing, and tapping. I was learning to feel it go fast and go slow, to feel how fast fast is from this slow and that. And just as I may move into a song at the remembered same tempo day after day, I've been going back and then forth and then back and then forth, and it's ready, and get set, and go wooosh into this, that, this, that, this, that. (50)

Sudnow goes on to detail his experiences learning the game, playing closely, and later deeply, as he begins to feel the game becoming an "instrumental extension of [his] body" (204). He plays obsessively, forgoing food and phone calls to dive deeper into understanding the system, comparing the experience to sport, music, and mathematics, and asking rhetorically, "Is this what they mean by the pleasure of mathematics, when numbers electrically tickle, torment, and torture your nerve endings?" (59).

Inspired by Sudnow, game journalist Brendan Keogh published a deep playthrough of the first-person shooter game *Spec Ops: The*

Line in the book *Killing is Harmless: A Critical Reading of Spec Ops: The Line* (2012). In it, Keogh calls his account a "reading" that tries to "understand just how I was so powerfully affected by it. For me, *The Line* made me question just what my responsibility is as a player of military shooters, and the following chapters are an exploration of *how* it made me ask those questions" (10). At the outset, Keogh recognizes the way in which *The Line* sets itself up as a game equivalent to Joseph Conrad's book *Heart of Darkness* (1899) or Francis Ford Coppola's film *Apocalypse Now* (1979). It is a game that uses the mechanics of a war game to question both the real mechanics of war and the play mechanics of virtual war—just as the game's literary and filmic references used the genre of war memoirs to question the effects of war on our memories and psyches. *The Line* begins as a "generic" shooter. We know what we're there to do, and we're not surprised when it's time to do it. During an early dialogue scene with a group of gunmen, Keogh explains that he knows the conversation is going nowhere. "I have played enough similar games to know that these negotiations are going to fail. I have played enough similar games to know I am going to shoot these men" (19).

With most games, Keogh says, you get an idea of what "kind" of game it is going to be fairly quickly: "With *The Line*, it is not that simple. It has a slow pay-off. It demands an investment with the promise that it will give a return later on. The opening chapters are only meaningful when the later chapters subvert the promises and expectations the opening chapters set up for the player—namely the promise that you will get to be a hero in this story" (21). Keogh's reading takes us through a game journey to the heart of darkness that, as he concludes in an understated fashion, does not have a good ending. Keogh's experience of the "generic" gameplay becomes deeply played as the situation becomes less and less "justifiable," as we move into a hallucinogenic experience of virtual violence in the extreme. At one point, he brutally kills a random soldier, hallucinating that the soldier is an enemy when in fact, he is not. But who is the enemy? Another character, seeing the assault, just comments, "Hey, it happens" (110). As if an accidental killing of a game character is a nonissue. Or is it friendly fire itself that is a nonissue? What is the game saying? How is Keogh responding? The end of his gameplay account brings Keogh hard up against the very nature of killing for entertainment. "It's not that I will stop playing shooters," he states, "but I will no longer be able to deny what I am truly doing in them" (158).

Capturing deep readings of games has been one of the goals of the Well Played talks at the annual Games for Change Festival, which are curated by games professor Drew Davidson. He also serves as the editor of the Well Played series of books, previously mentioned in chapter 2, published by ETC Press at Carnegie Mellon University. The forewords to each book frame the essays that make up each chapter as "in-depth close readings of video games that parse out the various meanings to be found in the experience of playing a game" (Davidson 2011, xi). The foreword goes on to explain the use of the term *well played* in two senses, the first of which is important here as it relates to being "well played" and being "well read." Specifically, the Well Played book series states that "well played is to games as well read is to books. So, a person who reads books a lot is 'well read,' and a person who plays games a lot is 'well played'" (Davidson 2011, xi). The second meaning of "'well played' [is] as in 'well done.' So, a hand of poker can be 'well played' by a person, and a game can be 'well played' by the development team" (Davidson 2011, xi). In some ways, our concept of deep play is both of these and, yet, neither of them. To play deeply is not necessarily to play "a lot" or to play widely. Sudnow's deep account of his play of *Breakout* was his first video game experience. He did play *Breakout* "a lot," but he did not play other games at all. He was, by the Well Played definition, not at all "well played." And, in many ways, he did not play the game very well at all. Much of his account is about failure to clear the screen. It becomes an obsession. He goes so far as to reach out to the developers and use his position as a journalist to get an interview where he grills them on how the code works—so that he can get better at playing and, hopefully, play a perfect game, which he never actually achieves. So, he is neither well played as a widely "read" player of games nor well played, as an expert player of *Breakout*. But there really is no question that his account, full of passion and obsession, detailed graphs, and evolving understanding, is an example of a player engaged in a deep relationship with a game.

The Well Played series produces a variety of "readings" of game—some of which are more typical academic approaches: an exploration of how *Pokémon* (The Pokémon Company 1996) teaches kids twenty-first-century skills, a collection of social and identity-focused research approaches to *World of Warcraft*, evaluations of the design solutions for games like *Chrono Trigger* (Square 1995) or *Street Fighter IV* (Capcom 1997). But quite often there are glimmers of what we would describe as deeply played experiences with games as texts. In Alice Taylor's (2011) reading of *Limbo* (Playdead 2010), she calls it—acknowledging the cliché—"the game that made me cry" (37). Why, she asks? "It might be because *Limbo* is so hard to play; maybe it was crying with relief," but that's not really why (Taylor 2011, 37). "*Limbo* is beautiful," she declares, "Haunting, melodious, atmospheric, sweet. Still somewhat macho, too, though, so as not to get too syrupy about it. The deaths are very brutal. The ragdoll physics of the little boy's body as he's hurled away by a monster, or cut into pieces by an advancing wood saw, or snapped into mush by a bear trap. It makes you physically wince. But then you respawn, and you go on" (40; figure 3.2). For those who have not played it, the game is a puzzle platformer where you play as a boy who wakes up in "limbo," that place between life and death, and must search for his sister. There are many thoughts—as many thoughts as there are players, really, about what this journey means. But in Taylor's reading, she says, "*I knew I was having a meaningful experience. . . .* I value those two hours of play over many ordinary things, as I

Figure 3.2
Limbo's atmospheric, but brutal, gameplay.

appear to remember them very clearly. I tangibly remember the sense of curiosity, the tiptoeing, the fear of the next death. I remember the crying, and I remember it with a sense of peacefulness and accomplishment" (41–42).

Taylor's description of her play of *Limbo* is one of several truly lovely accounts of deep play in *Well Played 3.0*. Another account in that volume can be found in José Zagal's (2011) reading of *Heavy Rain* (Quantic Dream 2010), when he begins by admitting he is nervous to play, writing, "My nervousness, as I began playing, was unusual. I've certainly been excited, even thrilled, about playing a new game. Never before had I been nervous" (56). Zagal discusses this reaction in relation to the player's responsibility to evoke the game experience, quoting Fullerton's playcentric design as part of the rhetoric that "places the player in the center, largely disconnected from the designer. How you interact with the game, what you make of it, how it should be experienced, are all placed squarely in the hands of the player" (2011, 56). As he plays, he feels formidable pressure from that responsibility: "I began to assume that everything mattered, somehow, and that I should take care with everything I did in the game, focusing on what I felt was right over what I felt the game's designer may have chosen to be 'right'" (58). Zagal's experience of pressure is created by *Heavy Rain*'s inclusion of so many different game verbs that the sheer variety becomes overwhelming. As Zagal notes, quoting writer F. Orca: "Players can toss a boomerang, rock a baby, or stove in heads with a wide selection of electrical appliances. *Heavy Rain* is a point-and-click adventure with a massive verb sheet. . . . Rather than making large choices every hour or so, the game has you constantly choosing every minute detail of these people's lives" (Zagal 2011, 58). But what really matters in Zagal's reading is not all the little activities; rather, it is the relationship between what he does and what he doesn't do, as well as the reasoning and meaning behind those choices to do or not to do something.

As we've already noted, Upton's (2017) situational play and the discussions around playcentric design that Zagal has quoted locate the essence of the game experience not in the input-output loop between player and game but rather in the game as understood—the player's personal grasp of the game, their mental model of its rules, consequences, meanings, and "*more*" that we discuss in chapter 1 (Upton 2017, 17). In Zagal's reading, that "more" includes what it means to be a father in a game. In *Heavy Rain*, we play as Ethan, whose eldest son dies in a car accident in the prologue of the game. This experience colors how Zagal, as a player, reacts to Ethan's surviving son, Shaun. He picks Shaun up from school and decides what to do next: snack, homework, dinner, bed. Nothing we do here really seems like it would make a difference to either character, but we know what is expected of us as the father in this scene. Zagal quotes Bogost in his description of Ethan making dinner for Shaun. "Ethan sits as Shaun eats, his pallid face staring at nothing. Time seems to pass, but the player must end the task by pressing up on the controller to raise Ethan from his chair. The silent time between sitting and standing offers one of the only powerful moments in the entire game" (Zagal 2011, 60; figure 3.3).

Figure 3.3
Ethan and Shaun at the dinner table in *Heavy Rain*.

What Bogost and Zagal are describing here is what Upton (2017) defines as *anticipatory play*, a type of gameplay when we are not focused on immediate play but rather on absorbing what has happened, what could happen, and what we would like to happen. This might be strategically or narratively. In a game like *Heavy Rain*, it means that the game is giving us time to decide how to be a father to Shaun after failing his brother. Zagal (2011) writes,

> This moment of silent contemplation only occurs because the player chooses not to act, to ignore the prompt that appears on the screen. It is a powerful and meaningful moment because of all that is left unsaid. Sticking to Shaun's schedule is simply going through the motions; what the player wants is for Ethan to somehow repair their relationship. To try something. Shaun's relationship with Ethan is so awkward and strained that the player desperately seeks a father-and-son moment that provides some hope for the future. (60)

In Upton's (2017) description of anticipatory play, he says it "takes time" and "requires stillness" (2). Like the moment at the dinner table, "We may spend minutes or even hours considering the consequences before we make a move" (Upton 2017, 2). Fullerton has spoken on this kind of play in her own games, *Walden, a game* (Fullerton and USC Game Innovation Lab 2017) and *The Night Journey* (Fullerton and Viola 2007), but also in games like the *Life Is Strange* series (Square Enix 2015–), which includes a similar mechanic for *noninteractive gameplay*—to use Upton's (2017, 28) term for what emerges when a game holds still but a player is still engaged deeply in contemplating the experience. In Fullerton's (2018) keynote at the Meaningful Play Conference, "Three Miles an Hour: Designing Games for the Speed of Thought," she describes such a noninteractive mechanic that, even with minimal player interaction, offers deep, anticipatory play in *Life Is Strange: Before the Storm* (Deck Nine 2017). Fullerton calls this the *interlude mechanic*, when "the game simply slows to a halt and allows you to process what has just happened, what might happen, and how you feel about it. You can choose to remain in these interludes for as long as you like, and they act like a kind of breathing space for you as a player, at times when the characters seem to need that space as well" (Fullerton 2018). Fullerton's example of the interlude mechanic comes from early in the game, where the main character, Chloe, is ditching school with the "cool girl," Rachel. Chloe doesn't know Rachel well but follows her on an adventure that will set in motion the rest of the game's story. They jump a ride on a train and, dangling their legs from the edge of a boxcar, sit in a somewhat uncomfortable silence. At this point, Chloe pulls out her music player and headphones. The player has the option to "Share with Rachel" or "Listen alone." If you share, each girl takes a headphone; if not, you put both headphones on yourself. The sequence that follows is best described as a music video. Mellow alt-rock music plays, and the game simply cuts between a series of angles of the girls, the train, the environment they are traveling through, glances that pass between them, and so on. It goes on for as long as the player does not choose to end it (figure 3.4). A similar interlude mechanic is found in the adventure

Figure 3.4
"Share with Rachel" or "Listen alone" in *Life Is Strange: Before the Storm.*

game *Marvel's Guardians of the Galaxy* (Eidos-Montréal 2021), where players have unlimited time to listen to a 1980s mixtape. Perhaps they also have nostalgia for that era's music as does the character Peter Quill, who longs for his childhood on Earth. These moments of "noninteractive" gameplay depend entirely on the level of engagement that the player brings to the experience for its meaning to be evoked. And the choice to keep it going can be seen as a measure of that engagement.

What are we playing at while we wait and do "nothing" in these seemingly noninteractive moments? In *Before the Storm,* we are playing with a kind of passive flirting. We're waiting for those glances, being in the moment with the girls as they flirt with each other and with the danger of skipping school and stealing a ride on a train. At other points in this game, and also in other games in the series, this same interlude mechanic is used to mark different types of emotional moments: to wind down after a particularly difficult experience and also to allow the characters—and through them, the players—to ponder the meanings of other character's actions, their intents, and possible outcomes of a situation. But is this really deep play? It is far from the obsessive involvement of Sudnow with the mechanics of *Breakout*, of Keogh's deeply felt shift in his relationship to shooters, or of Lantz's feeling of *Serpentes* shining a dim light into the normally invisible machinery of the brain. Fullerton notes that the interludes of *Life Is Strange* are so underrated by game enthusiasts that the sequences are not even mentioned in walkthroughs of the game. They are just assumed to be cutscenes of sorts that require no explanation or mention. But as Bogost asserts about the dinner scene in *Heavy Rain*, these interlude scenes in *Before the Storm* that require us to do nothing—or rather, to choose to do nothing—are meaningful moments of gameplay. If we choose to sit at the dinner table with Shaun, contemplating what life has become for these characters in the wake of tragedy and what still lies in wait for them, that is a deeply played moment of what Upton (2017) calls noninteractive gameplay. If we choose, in *Before the Storm*, to lie in bed smoking after a rough night out where we got in a fight with local bullies, we are playing our character differently—perhaps more deeply—than if we choose to jump up and greet the morning.

These emotionally complex moments in the *Life Is Strange* series may be ignored by game walkthrough websites that mainly focus on helping players navigate strategically difficult parts of games so that they can complete challenges. But they are not ignored by players who have documented their interludes: hours of footage can be found on YouTube showing the characters riding the train, lying in bed, or staring out at the ocean, wondering where the journey will take them. These moments are meaningful to players who have invested deeply in the game. These players are capturing and posting those moments to share what has moved them so deeply in their play. As Upton (2017) writes, "Anticipatory play is not merely exploratory, it's also constructive, and it is the constructive aspect of the experience that gives it much of its depth and power" (53). The result of anticipatory play, and a deeply felt reaction to it, is not,

Upton claims, "a change in the game's external state, but a shift in our internal constraints" (52). By this, he means our own game as understood—our mental model of what is going on. This might result in a change in our plan—what we think we should do next, our emotional strategy, our prediction of what will happen next, or our interpretation of why things are happening the way that they are. Interpretations, importantly, are an often-ignored part of deep play. Beyond how deeply we understand a game system, how we respond to choices presented by it, and how we make plans and formal strategies to beat it, deep play is also about interpreting our experiences within it.

Upton describes *interpretive play* as a convergence of narrative and gameplay, and it does seem clear that the examples of deep play above go beyond the exploration of mechanics and are moments when the activities, or verbs, of gameplay intertwine purposefully and effectively with the *beats* of the narrative. The concept of beats comes to us from theater and film, where the term refers to a shift in the story, however minuscule. A beat could mean that a character makes a realization, changing their understanding of a situation, or a beat could mean a decision, where a character changes their objective in a scene. Beats can be private or public moments, but they are usually moments that are underscored by some kind of storytelling technique that cues the audience to pay attention because something is about to change. Upton, in adapting the term for use in describing interactive beats, determines that a "beat must contain some degree of ambiguity to feel playful. If the meaning of a beat is completely obvious, then it won't provide any narrative play" (90). On the other hand, he warns that "this ambiguity needs to be bounded. If a beat is too open-ended, if there are too many ways to interpret it, then our resulting confusion will cause play to collapse" (91). He compares the interpretation of narrative beats in games to those in reading, calling out the several types of narrative ambiguity that readers can "play" with, including grammatical (what a word means), syntactical (what a sentence means), motivational (what this means to a character), logistical (what happened), thematic (what this is about), and contextual (what the author means). We can break down these types of beats to see that logistical beats are somewhat efferent in nature, whereas grammatical and syntactical beats relate strongly to our close reading of verbs of play. Motivational, thematic, and contextual beats take us into the realm of deeper readings, where the questions of why something has happened, how it happened, what might happen next, as well as what it means to the characters, the story, and theme of the game are the most pertinent questions.

To use our example of the *Before the Storm* scene, the player's choice of whether to "Share with Rachel" or "Listen alone" is primarily a logistical beat: it determines what happens. However, it has motivational overtones—whether we choose to share our music with Rachel says something about how the player feels about the girls' relationship. Because of this, the seemingly noninteractive sequence that follows carries those motivational overtones as well while we think about what our choice meant—what Upton would call a syntactical beat. As the sequence plays out, giving us time to absorb the moment, we can fall into the realm of thematic and contextual beats: What is this story about? What does the author want us to learn from this story? In other words, we can begin the deeper process of interpreting the beats of the gameplay during this slow sequence of supposedly noninteractive play, and because we choose when it ends, we can take as much time as we need to go through this process. By its very nature, the interlude mechanic supports an aesthetic reading of this game. If we were only playing efferently, we would choose to end the sequence immediately, jumping quickly past the interlude and on to the next choice point or logistical beat, skipping all other aesthetic aspects of this game. When viewed in this way, we can see that the inability of game enthusiasts to recognize the challenge of these sequences is, in fact, a lack of literacy in the realm of game aesthetics. Players who do not or cannot recognize game beats beyond the logistical may be unable or unwilling to play aesthetically.

Looking back to Mariam Karis Cronin's discussion of literacy as the basis for literature, we can see that the current hyperfocus on games as systems has, in some ways, blinded us to the power of a more integrated view of games as holistic aesthetic experiences. In this way, we have, to paraphrase Cronin's words, become too focused on the foundational literacy of games (deep play of their systems) at the expense of the literacy skills that literature demands (deep play of the full range of the gameplay experience). Cronin (2014) warns us that a society that does so "would be shallow and dispassionate" (46). Upton (2017) echoes the problematic nature of dividing these types of literacy in his description of interpretive play, saying that this more inclusive concept, "gives us a powerful tool for negotiating the overlap between game and story. Instead of treating gameplay and narrative as two independent systems that are uncomfortably yoked together, we can instead analyze them as two manifestations of a unified play process" (96). However, Upton emphasizes that this unified play process depends on the approach of the player. He states that, because of this,

> situational design is intended not only as a methodology for designing games but also as a *manifesto for playing them* [emphasis ours]. The acknowledgment of the existence of these implicit goals gives us a way to re-conceptualize what we're doing when we play a game. Instead of being trapped within a game-centric system that ascribes significance to our moves only to the extent that they help us win, we can understand our moves within a broader player-centric system that accommodates a wider range of motivations. (96)

Echoing our initial concept of the well-read game, Upton (2017) concludes, "There are valid things to do with games besides trying to win them, and those other things often can move and transform us in ways that winning cannot" (96).

An example of a game that relies completely on this type of interpretive play in the design of its core mechanics is *Walden, a game,* by Fullerton. In *Walden,* the player, who takes on the role of philosopher and author Henry David Thoreau, is tasked with living in the woods simply, like Thoreau. They must find food and fuel as well as make and maintain shelter and clothing to satisfy their basic physical needs. This set of tasks is structured as a light but typical set of survival mechanics. You can chop wood or pick up driftwood for fuel. Pick berries, fish, or grow beans for food. Mend your clothes and build and repair your cabin. All these activities are generally familiar to game players, who are often faced with the challenge of maintaining the health and safety of a character. Where *Walden, a game* differs in its mechanics is that there is a second set of activities that are hinted at but not explicitly described. These activities include seeking solitude, interacting with the creatures of the woods, listening to the sounds of society and technology, but at a distance, and reading inspirational texts that can be found in the forest and nearby in Ralph Waldo Emerson's library. Discovering these activities and exploring the woods to find other hidden moments, special items, quests, and connections to nature make up the other "half" of the character's well-being that must be considered (see figure 3.5). The juxtaposition of familiar game activities like maintaining physical health against the challenge of discovering and maintaining the more elusive well-being associated with "inspiration" in the game provides a unique opportunity for deep and interpretive play. As one Steam player wrote, "I found myself living the game, as if I was really there and had to do all that survival stuff, had to THINK like someone living alone in the woods. Then, it was as if I shifted back in time as if I was actually feeling his presence or feeling MY presence in HIS time" (Tekodda 2020, para. 4).

Walden, a game asks the player not to "win" at a game of survival but to interpret the small moments of Thoreau's life in the woods and discover how to understand his experience. Another

Figure 3.5
Seeking inspiration on the pond in *Walden, a game*.

player says, "Walden asks the player to think about life, existence, meaning, connectedness. . . . In my first playthrough, I learned of Thoreau's family's loss, the death of John, of the plans Henry had with John and how they were cut short due to the death, and I learned of Henry (and John) being rejected by Ellen Sewall through her father, etc. So then, it seemed a double whammy when [Emerson's] young [son] also tragically died. . . . The lack of a sound effect and no money given when picking up toys on the day of the death caused me to question whether I just broke the game for a split second, but then I realized what had happened." This player built an interpretation of Thoreau's mindset through experiences he had in the game, such as cleaning up Emerson's son's toys after the boy's tragic death around the same time as Thoreau's own brother's passing. The player asks himself as he writes, "Am I correct in interpreting that Thoreau partly decided to do this grand experiment as a coping mechanism for depression after his brother's death? Did it precipitate everything? his austerity, his solitude, his needing to find himself and his place in the world?" The player has evoked meaning from a moment of gameplay: the picking up of toys, which has been designed to change in its reward loop on the day we learn of the child's death. Where once we, as Thoreau, were paid to help the Emerson family clean up after the child, now we do it to spare the family the grief of seeing toys scattered around the house. This change in the gameplay spurred the player to interpret and realize something larger about the narrative situation and to perform this task not as a player, but as a friend to the grieving Emersons, and for no extrinsic reward but simply the knowledge that it was related to Thoreau's own grief about the loss of his brother.

What can we make of gameplay such as this? That is, experiences that intentionally invite us to go beyond the deep play of systemic interaction; experiences that, like literature's, invite our interpretation through ambiguous narrative play as well as the performance of dramatic situations. These are experiences that cannot be played or won in any traditional sense. They must be performed as we would perform our part in a theatrical play, felt deeply as we would feel in acting out such a part, and "won" only in the sense that we have the sense of grasping new meanings through our play. The depth of our response in these cases can evoke a performance of sorts that goes beyond our traditional understanding of why we play.

4
Performing a Game

Play theorists have long argued about how and why we play as well as how to define it. Roger Caillois's influential essay *Les Jeux et les Hommes* (1958), published in English as *Man, Play, and Games*, presents one of the earliest unified theories of play. In it, Caillois categorizes play into four main types, each characterized by distinct attributes and tendencies: *agôn* (competition), *alea* (randomness or chance), *mimicry* (role-play, make-believe), and *ilinx* (disorientation). He further contrasts two extremes, or polarities, of play: *ludus*, which is rule-based, structured, and organized, and *paidia*, where play is imaginative, make-believe, and unstructured. When we engage in competitive rule-based play, such as chess or *Halo*, we experience one form of game. But when we engage in role-play and imaginative or unstructured play, we open another realm of possible play experiences. This realm of possibilities includes the idea that our play can be a performance of sorts. As with an actor taking on a role or a musician pouring their emotions into the performance of a piece, our motivations as we play a game can become so intertwined with those of a player character that we virtually lose ourselves in them. When this happens, our reading of a game can take on the aspect of a performance.

The ability to lose ourselves in play begins early in our development as players. As part of his broader theory of cognitive development, Swiss psychologist Jean Piaget (1962) proposes a theory of play that emphasizes the role of play in children's intellectual development. He categorizes play into several stages, each corresponding to different developmental levels. As children grow, they develop new cognitive abilities and concepts, contributing to their overall schema or mental-model understanding of the world. First to emerge are *practice games*, which are not rule-based. Practice games include rough-and-tumble play, a play pattern that is also observable in the animal kingdom. Around ages two through six, children begin to play *symbolic games*, which begin as imaginative fantasy. As children reach adolescence, this fantasy play becomes more theatrical and begins to involve role-play reenactments (Piaget 1962). Piaget observed that children may grow out of role-play, stating that "games of make-believe may become games with rules" (1962, 145); however, we do not necessarily see this with today's modern video games. Although the role-playing video games that today's adults play are rule-based, they are also deeply imaginative, involving the same kind of fantasy play and dramatic reenactments that hark back to childhood. And, though the themes may be more mature and the social interactions more complex, role-play activates adult emotions as deeply as it does for children, giving opportunities to live out fantasies and rehearse situations that we might otherwise never face in our real-world encounters.

As mentioned in chapter 2, Soviet psychologist Lev Vygotsky's (1967, 1978) sociocultural learning theory posits that children develop social skills during play when they are supported by more capable peers or players (Vygotsky 1967, 1978). Vygotsky's concept of *sociodramatic play* encourages individuals to create and act out imaginary scenarios. This kind of play, also known as make-believe, pretend play, or imaginative play, evolves and changes as children grow into adulthood, reflecting a greater cognitive, social, and emotional development, but it does not disappear (Vygotsky 1967, 1978). In early childhood, sociodramatic play is characterized by simple scenarios, such as playing house, pretending to be animals, or taking on the roles of favorite characters. This form of sociodramatic play is common in children's museums and early childhood classrooms, where young children dress up and pretend to take on the roles of adults, playing as doctors, teachers, or chefs. As children enter middle childhood (around seven to eleven years old), they may develop more elaborate storylines involving multiple characters and intricate scenarios. Next, in adolescence (around eleven to eighteen years old), more abstract forms of imaginative thinking emerge, where children may be drawn to activities such as role-playing games, creative writing, and children's theater. In late adolescence and adulthood, sociodramatic play can transform into activities like more traditional theater, improvisational acting, and storytelling, each of which offers opportunities for exploring emotions, different viewpoints, and social dynamics (Vygotsky 1967, 1978). As with the books we read, the types of themes and storylines we play may evolve and change, but our interest and need for sociodramatic play remain an important part of our lives as we grow and mature. And, as we will see, our ability to take on make-believe roles and motivations and to play as the characters we control in games can be an important aspect of reading many types of games.

Play theorist Brian Sutton-Smith, whom we mention in chapter 1, critiques Piaget's assertions that children's play is imitative and serves solely as a function of intellectual and cognitive growth (1966). To Sutton-Smith (1966, 1997)—as well as to many modern play theorists—human play has its roots in evolutionary adaptations. Hide-and-seek, tag, and tossing a ball are more than play and games; these activities reflect how humans hunted and evaded predators. In other words, we are hardwired for play patterns that prepare us for challenges that humans previously faced in our collective hunter-gatherer past (Gray 2017). Play is a rehearsal for situations that we must be prepared to face in the future. Today, those situations may be emotional as well as physical and intellectual, and, as we will see, may involve sociodramatic play at all age levels and in states that may or may not be immediately recognizable as play by an observer.

In his book *The Ambiguity of Play* (1997), Sutton-Smith describes seven *rhetorics of play*, which explore the way that play can be seen in the context of different value systems, which include progress, fate, power, identity, imaginary, self, and frivolity (Sutton-Smith 1997, 8). In chapter 1 we note that our focus on the subjectivity of the individual at play is deeply aligned with the rhetoric of self, but we can also find connections to his broader list of play activities that range from "the mostly more private to the mostly more public" (5). For example, reading books can be seen as *solitary play* as we interpret our transactions with a written text. Texts can also engage readers in the kind of *vicarious play* that engages us as audiences when we bring fictional worlds to life in our imaginations (Sutton-Smith 1997). Sutton-Smith's work invites a comparison between reading books and playing games by noting that "video games and computer play" are, like books, examples of solitary play (123). This comparison extends to the observation of various types of solitary play. Observing a reader may not tell us how they are transacting with the book; only the reader themselves can define the type of experience they are having and determine whether it is playful. By extension, only a player can tell us how they are transacting with a game and whether it is an imaginative or emotional experience.

Sutton-Smith challenges rigid demarcations around various types of play, observing that play is flexible and open to various interpretations by participants. Importantly, he claims that outside spectators cannot determine whether an activity is play, as it is subjective and can be best determined only by players. So we can be playing imaginatively at any time in any place, and only we as individuals may know or understand that we are playing. Our internal lives of play are bounded by our own consciousness that we are performing playful acts. When we watch others playing games, we cannot always see the depth of experience they are having by simple observation. As many parents know, a child playing a video game may seem to be doing "nothing," whereas from their own perspective, they are having a deeply emotional and intellectual experience. They are, as we have seen from several player readings already, performing important deeds and learning new ideas. As with reading books, this kind of *mind or subjective play*—play activities that also include daydreaming and other fantasizing—which may seem from the outside to be passive or lacking activity, may actually be quite active as the reader or player evokes a fully realized world and performs within it. There are opportunities, like book clubs, that offer *informal social play*, where readers have opportunities to unpack and share what they experienced with others (Sutton-Smith 1997). And, as we suggest in chapter 8, this same model could provide an appropriate way for players to similarly unpack their experiences with games.

Sutton-Smith uses the example of the classic tabletop role-playing game *Dungeons & Dragons* (Wizards of the Coast 1974) to show how games, like reading, can offer subjective play, as well as vicarious play and *play as performance*. Sutton-Smith's play as performance is particularly interesting to us because of the way in which it integrates reader response with player interactivity. For Sutton-Smith, play as performance is a broad concept, encompassing various forms of creative and imaginative play, not limited to structured games or rule-based activities. Beyond games, other examples of play as performance include "playing the piano, playing music, being a play actor, playing the fishes, playing the horses, play voices, playhouses" (Sutton-Smith 1997, 5). This type of play emphasizes the symbolic and expressive aspects of play, highlighting how play allows individuals to explore different identities, emotions, and ideas in a safe and imaginative context. Performative play can include a wide range of activities, from children pretending to be superheroes to adults engaging in theatrical performances to role-playing games. When we play performatively, we align our motivations with those identities we are taking on and play within the constraints of that world, learning and rehearsing ways to be in that world. Like an actor in a theatrical play, we are reading our "lines," but we are living the part as well. When we are aligned with the motivations of a player character, as we will see in a moment, the aesthetic reading that is evoked can be heightened immensely and can challenge and broaden our perspective of the world within and outside the game.

A good example of a player's performance in a video game can be seen in the following scene from *Before the Storm*. In this scene, the characters are putting on a school play, Shakespeare's *Tempest*, and Rachel, the popular cool girl at school already described in chapter 3, is playing the lead, Prospero. When a huge fire keeps the actress playing Ariel from getting to the theater, the player character, Chloe, must step in and take on the role (see figure 4.1). As Fullerton experienced when playing the game as Chloe:

> I'm suddenly thrown into a strange costume of bird feathers and a beaked mask and given a script to read quickly to prepare. Um, it's a game, so I don't read thoroughly; I just flip through the pages. I see the yellow highlights for Ariel's lines, but not realizing what is coming next, I don't take the time to read or memorize it. I figure there will be a way to refer to the script in the moment. Then it's time for the performance. They practically shove me on stage. The lights are blinding when I choose to look at them. Rachel is performing perfectly. She calls to me and asks me a question: Did I bring a storm on the ship of her enemies as she asked me? My choices are varied. One is clearly wrong, "Yea, the most pointiest Tempest ever . . ." is definitely not what Shakespeare would have written. But the other two are possible: "I wrought a storm . . ." and "I boarded the King's ship . . ." could both be Shakespeare. I choose the latter and give a speech about boarding and burning the ship. Aside from a few coughs in the audience, it seems to be okay. I'm relieved; maybe I

Figure 4.1
Chloe and Rachel perform onstage in *Life Is Strange: Before the Storm.*

> can get through this without too many mistakes! But the choices get harder, and the audience starts coughing and murmuring at one point. The stage manager in the wings looks distraught, but then suddenly Rachel joins me in improvisation! She asks me why I want my freedom from her, kneels before me as the audience rustles louder in surprise, and begs me to stay with her: "Spirit, take my hands, most faithful friend. For but a little longer, I beseech, continue in thy service to my schemes. And when they are complete, I swear to thee, we shall fly beyond this isle—the corners of the world are mere prologue." The audience is suddenly with us, even as we verge further from the actual lines of the play. Even the stage manager congratulates me on my "transformational" performance.

The scene turns out very different from Shakespeare's version—though it brings his subtext of a potential love relationship between Prospero and Ariel to the surface, as it surfaces the same potential for a relationship between Rachel and Chloe. The design choice to give the player the script beforehand, knowing that they won't memorize it perfectly, sets up the feeling that we are failing as a player. As Fullerton journals,

> Even though I know what I'm supposed to do, and I was given everything I needed to do it perfectly, I am left standing in the blinding lights, unable to remember my lines, and am finally saved by my friend, who steps slightly out of her character to make the scene work. I feel so moved by the moment. It reminds me of a time when I had to take an acting class, and even though I'm very shy, I was able to lose myself in a part one day. It opened up an understanding of what it really meant to act. This feels the same way. The cooperative improv play with Rachel allows me to feel what I know Chloe's character is supposed to be feeling—a sense of success as a performer and a sense of exhilaration as the relationship with Rachel takes a step forward.

Many narrative games, including the *Life Is Strange* series, explicitly adopt the visual and structural language of theater and cinema when they want to signal to players that the game is meant to be played with attention to story and performance. In *Life Is Strange,* each game is set in "episodes," and within each episode are clearly recognizable scenes. We walk into the school auditorium in *Before the Storm,* and the scene begins when we get there. It's as if the other performers were waiting for us to arrive on our mark before beginning. As in a film or theatrical play, the scene is an important moment of the story, and we need to be there to see it occur. We are not referring to "cut scenes" here or interludes that players simply watch, but rather scripted game events that are triggered by player actions, similar to traditional game events but less about challenge progression than narrative progression. In many ways, these kinds of game scenes and episodes lend themselves to thinking about reading games as immersive theater experiences, where the audience may be included as part of the play. In an immersive theater experience like that in *Sleep No More* (Punchdrunk 2011), for example, the audience follows the performers around a five-story building in New York City, which has been set dressed to create all the locations for an adaptation of Shakespeare's *Macbeth.* The castle of Macbeth, the Birnam wood, the witches' cavern, and so on, are all wanderable within the building. As the actors play out the story, the audience chooses to follow any of them that catches their interest, sometimes being drawn aside by an actor for an intimate one-on-one performance.

Theater scholar Suzy Woltmann (2023) connects the social and playful interactions of immersive theater to the work of French literary theorist and philosopher Roland Barthes, who discusses the concept of the *writerly text* (*texte scriptable* in French) in his 1967 essay *The Death of the Author* as translated by Stephen Heath in *Image, Music, Text* (1977) and elaborates on it in his book *S/Z* (1970). A writerly text differs from a *readerly text,* which affords readers an opportunity to engage passively with passages that may have more of a fixed meaning. Comparatively, a writerly text invites the reader to participate in the construction of meaning by offering multiple layers of interpretation and allowing for various readings. Writerly texts are open-ended and can lack a fixed or single interpretation, where the reader becomes a cocreator of meaning, as the text itself is open to multiple interpretations, reinterpretations, and personal connections. Woltmann relates this to immersive theater because improvisation is essential and actors—and sometimes audience members—coauthor the experience together. When Fullerton "played" *Sleep No More,* she had a visceral interactive experience chasing the mad King Macbeth through the forest. She journaled the moment:

> The trees smell like pine, and they are moving. The actor is running quickly through them, and I am just trying to keep up. My breath catches in the white mask that the audience members all have to wear during the performance. It is hot and wet as it blows back on my face. I almost trip as I weave in and out of the trees, crowded by other audience members who are also desperate to follow the mad king. Suddenly, he falls to his knees in front of me and looks directly at me with a wild stare. We make eye contact for a moment as I stop, shocked, and almost fall on him as I come up short. It is so intense that I become afraid of him and draw back just an inch or two. But the actor behind the king's eyes sees my fear and shifts his gaze. He

> grabs the hand of someone else off to my left and drags them out of the forest. I am so disappointed. I want so badly, now that the moment has passed, to have been chosen by the madman, but I froze in that instant and lost my chance. I feel an intense sense of failure. As if I have lost a game within the play.

Barthes (1977, 153) envisions the reader as an active participant with a text who "writes it anew" through the act of reading, and we see this clearly in our own readings of games and equally in the immersive theater experience *Sleep No More*. Games and media studies professor Sarah Stang does not agree. Citing scholars such as Chris Crawford (2000), who, as discussed in chapter 1, presents a cybernetic view of games' interactivity, and Barthes's concepts of writerly texts, she writes, "Indeed, no matter how loudly a videogame proclaims its own interactivity, it does not allow for co-authorship" (Stang 2019, para. 7). In other words, different from improvisational acting in immersive theater and live-action role-playing games (LARPs), Stang feels that video games have a more restricted possibility space, with predetermined pathways and feedback loops. She uses the term *faux-scriptible* text to describe how games with predetermined outcomes give an "illusion of meaning, power, and active participation" (Charles 2009, 289, as quoted by Stang 2019, para. 8). Stang's argument, however, is based on the classic cybernetic concept of player-game exchange, rather than seeing the "game" not as an object itself but as an evocation created by a player's individual experience. As we described in chapter 1, reading games aesthetically allows for a much broader interpretation of player agency.

When we view games through the lens of reader response and situational play, we see that the readings created by players across written texts and performed texts, including books, games, and immersive theater experiences, are not essentially different. Each of these, as the readings shared from *Life Is Strange* and *Sleep No More*, cast the reader/player in a performative role. Whether or not they can change the outcome, as in Stang's measure of "co-authorship," is not the critical question. The question is better framed as whether a player's reading of a text "writes it anew," to use Barthes's (1977, 153) measure of a writerly text. And this, we propose, is a matter of how "open" a text is to allowing players to evoke their own readings. Whereas the example from *Life Is Strange* is one of a game that is "on rails"—meaning that the player has limited ability to change the outcome—it still allows for an emotional performance by the player. It does not actively make room for the player to write their own experiences, and yet the player finds a way to do so. The *Sleep No More* example is perhaps a more "open" text in that it does not dictate an "on rails" experience for the audience. In this particular immersive experience, the audience is free to roam and to engage or not engage with the play as presented. In fact, when Fullerton went back for several other performances, she saw completely different scenes each time. One time, she just wandered the empty sets of one floor when there were no performers there, eating from candy jars in the set for Hecate's apothecary with another mischievous and anonymous audience member.

As we see in chapter 7, however, when we discuss oppositional play, the openness of a text, though perhaps lending itself to more complex writerly experiences, does not negate the possibility of player responses to what Barthes would call a readerly text. The openness of a text is not determined by its aesthetic form—video game, immersive theater, book, and so on—but by the formality of its narrative structure. Just as a novel like *Ulysses* (Joyce 1920) can be seen as a writerly experience because of its narrative structure—evolving from its more traditional opening chapters into a deeply complex stream of consciousness by the end of the book—so, too, can a video game like *Walden, a game*, as described in chapter 3, be seen as writerly because of its similarly open narrative structure. Exploratory narrative games like *Walden* allow the player to follow their own cues and impulses, much as open texts like *Ulysses* allow the reader to evoke their own thoughts as they follow the wandering thoughts of the characters in the book. When we walk through the woods of *Walden*, playing at being Thoreau, and pick up an arrowhead, we hear the character's thoughts played as a voice-over, but we also think our own thoughts, evoking our own reading of the experience. Similarly, when reading about walking along the seashore with Stephen Dedalus in *Ulysses*, hearing the sounds of the water, and his thoughts of his mother's death, we can follow along with his inner monologue, but we are also evoking our own reading of the experience. The nature of an open text is not bounded by whether an experience is generated by a game, a book, a play, or an immersive experience but by whether we are able, within its narrative confines, to evoke our own experiences, our own aesthetic reading, beyond the constraints of the basic authorial intent. Freedom to play and to perform is the true defining characteristic, in our perspective, of the writerly text.

Freedom, Safety, and Performative Play

So what does this all mean for the potential of performative play and reading games aesthetically? What can we learn from applying the concepts of performative play to the reading of games? Evolutionary psychologist Peter Gray builds on the work of Piaget, Vygotsky, and Sutton-Smith in his current studies of mixed-age, self-directed play. Gray's book *Free to Learn* (2013) characterizes play at all ages as a creative act that often leads to fantasy play, as players create characters and storylines. The symbolic and expressive aspects of play highlight how individuals can explore different identities, emotions, and ideas in a safe and imaginative context. Like Sutton-Smith's, Gray's (2017, 2023) definition of play entails not just these characteristics; rather, it is a confluence of several imaginative practices.

Freedom for performative play requires safety for the players—physical and psychological. And this sense of safety derives from one of the most well-known concepts in game studies—that of the magic circle. The *magic circle* is a term from Johann Huizinga's book *Homo Ludens: A Study of the Play-Element in Culture* (1955). In it, he describes a symbolic boundary that encompasses the space and time of a game or play activity. Within this "circle," players willingly suspend their ordinary reality and adopt the rules and roles defined by the game. It is a temporary, voluntary escape from the real world into a realm where the game's structure and objectives take precedence, creating a distinct and immersive experience. Huizinga (1955) writes,

> All play moves and has its beginning within a playground marked off beforehand, either materially or ideally . . . the arena, the card table, the magic circle, the temple, the stage, the screen, the court of justice, etc., are all in form and function playgrounds, i.e., forbidden spots, isolated, hedged round, within which special rules obtain. All are temporary worlds within the ordinary world, dedicated to the performance of an act apart. (10)

Once we are within the magic circle, bound by the rules of play, we are free to perform actions that we would otherwise never consider—for example, killing, betrayal—but we are also free to perform actions we would like to think ourselves capable of and may never have had the chance to face, such as courage in the face of untenable odds, sacrifice, loyalty, and difficult decision-making. In this way, play within the temporary world of a game encourages self-knowledge and self-reflection. Other arts also create their own temporary worlds, like the frame of a painting, a motion picture screen, or the proscenium of a stage. The invitation to enter these worlds is also ritualized in particular moments of transition: the dimming of the lights, the drawing back of the curtains, the opening words of a novel, and, for games, the invitation to play. And when we are freed by entry into these temporary worlds, we can take on the kind of identity and role-play that Gray and Sutton-Smith describe at any age.

As an example, we can look at *Stray* (BlueTwelve Studio 2022), a video game where players take on the role of a stray cat. Set in a cyberpunk-inspired world, humans seem to have disappeared, leaving behind plants, robots, and Zurks, mutated bug-like enemies that swarm players. *Stray* offers a unique perspective on how a feline creature and a companion robot drone might interact with a futuristic world. Through an evolutionary lens, the imaginative play in the game involves risky behaviors, such as running and hiding from enemies. Controlling the cat avatar has some of the same affordances as acting on a stage. As with many video games, a game's fiction is embodied through play (Gray 2017).

Performing as a stray cat, players navigate a sprawling cityscape, solving various puzzles and uncovering the secrets of this enigmatic world. Communicating and making alliances with robots is essential for progressing through the narrative. B-12 is the cat's companion robot drone that translates signs and dialogue with other robots. The narrative is also revealed through "memories" that are "remembered" by B-12 as the cat explores the city (see figure 4.2). Like the arrowheads in *Walden*, each memory offers a scrap of perspective on the narrative world. The memories of B-12 are put together by the player as part of a layering of narrative and experience that provokes wondering about the past and anticipation about what will happen.

As Farber played, he journaled his experience:

> I am wandering through the slums of Dead City, encountering robots, some of whom water plants and play guitar and weave blankets. I am reminded of Meow Wolf, the immersive art space that has a similar cyberpunk aesthetic. These are the slower parts of the game, which I prefer. I can take my time, performing and leaping around as a cat would. I have never owned a cat, just dogs. I sometimes am prompted to curl up on a rug or scratch at a wall; playing as a cat is strangely satisfying. Seemingly goalless, I wander the city's streets and climb up its buildings by jumping from exterior air conditioner units. But I do have a goal, a purpose in my mind.

Figure 4.2
Memories unlocked by the robot drone B-12 in *Stray*.

> I meet Momo, a robot who gives me a quest: he needs to recover notebooks from his long-lost friends Clementine, Zbaltazar, and Doc. Do robots have friends? Why do robots write in paper notebooks? Before I leap back out of his windows, I explore his bedroom. I walk through a beaded curtain door. Why do robots have bedrooms? I encounter a wall with a poster for something called Back Home 2. The game prompts me that this is a "Memory." I click the button, and my drone robot helper B-12 flies up, and a dialogue box opens. "Oh, Back Home 2. I remember this video game. It was made just after I was created, I think? I can't remember it well. The scientist and I spent a lot of time playing it. It was fun. I miss him. Why can't I remember his name?" And that's it. New Memory Uncovered is displayed on the screen, with one of the open slots now filled. Who was B-12? I let this memory linger, thinking about other ones that I have found so far. How old is B-12? Why am I the only cat here? Why do sentient robots live in futuristic slums? What happened to the humans?

As with many of the game readings we have shared, the performative play of *Stray* encompasses more than what we control on a screen. In this playthrough, Farber played as a cat but also with the bits of narrative he had to assemble in his mind, which motivated him to ask questions about his "life" as a cat. Games, like plays and novels, create motivations for players that drive their desires for how the play will unfold. Farber only received bits of unlocked memories, which he had to interpret as he played, but they led him to wonder and explore and even to playact like a cat. He purred and meowed and scratched his claws on carpets and walls. In one location, he jumped onto the keys of a piano, playing as he walked—an explicit example of Sutton-Smith's (1977) play as performance. *Stray* invited Farber to cross into the magic circle, where he could "be" a cat. He knew that leaping off a building as a cat would not affect him in the real world, so it was safe to explore in a way that only a cat could explore that world. In some ways, a video game like *Stray* provides a safe space for an adult to playact as a cat that a child would not need. A child might just get down on the floor, roll around, and purr without the need for narrative or the pretense of a game. An adult may need the permission of a game like *Stray* to enter the safety of a space where they can fully engage in role-playing as a cat.

But what of games that explore worlds that are not safe, even for the player characters? Can we still play and perform when there is a sense of real danger, even potentially triggering emotional danger for players? To explore that question, we can look at several readings from another game. *What Remains of Edith Finch* (Giant Sparrow 2017) tells the story of the doomed Finch family from the perspective of Edith, the last remaining member. The story begins when she returns to explore her family's mysterious and tragic history in their large and abandoned house. Presented as a collection of short stories, players act out various family members' lives and their deaths. Its narrative intentionally lacks a single, authoritative interpretation; for instance, it is never revealed whether the Finch family was actually cursed or just unfortunate.

Played in the first-person camera, character faces are only seen in photographs and drawings, and their distinct hands and feet are seen from the player's first-person point of view. *Edith Finch* combines exploration, environmental storytelling, and magic realism to create an emotionally resonant experience. It borrows the structure of short story collections bound together with a common theme—in this case, familial secrets. The short stories use literary devices throughout to provoke powerful emotions. These emotions are experienced as the game is performed, as players are invited to cross the proscenium on to the stage of play. When Farber played as Gus Finch, he journaled the following:

> I enter another bedroom in the Finch house. I see a makeshift shrine at the foot of a bed with a photo of a young boy, white extinguished candles, a photo of a kite in the air, and a spool of kite line with a note wrapped around it. This is Gus Finch's shrine. On the table it states, "Gus 1969–1982." I will be playing Gus's final moments. On the screen, near the spool, is an icon of a journal. The picture of the kite, the spool, and the dates of Gus's life foreshadow what is about to occur. I click it, and the note unfurls. "A Poem for Gus" begins. "Who always said the wedding was a bad idea," I see and hear. The screen turns black.
>
> The scene changes. I am now Gus, flying a kite at a rocky beach. I—as Gus—am flying a kite into a storm. Tables and chairs and a wedding tent are farther down the beach, closer to the water. My father is getting remarried. Written and narrated by his sister Dawn Finch, I see words appear in the sky, near the kite. "Our father never hit us kids, at least not very hard," the poem began. "Before the day my brother said with teenage disregard. That he'd be dead before he'd see a wedding in our yard." When I move the spool to hit the lines and stanzas, the words are collected into an amalgam of letters that now trail behind the kite's tail.
>
> A storm gathers in the sky. "My father made him come, of course, but Gus stood far apart; Just flew his kite and bottled up the storm inside his heart," the poem later reads. In addition to the words, the tail of the kite catches chairs and objects from the wedding scene. At one point, I give the middle finger to the wedding scene as my kite flies. "The wind picked up and panicked geese appeared and quickly went. But all that the humans did that day was go inside the tent," the poem continues. More objects are swept up, including the tent.

> Then I am wiped away. "I wish that I could truly say I thought about you on that day. Out there on the beach alone, just you, the wind, the sea, and foam, But I didn't. Until we found you," the poem concludes. I am gone into the darkness. Gus is now gone. I am back at the foot of the bed. I put the spool down, and the poem—the elegy—is over.

Edith Finch is a difficult game to perform. It puts the player into the role of each doomed family member in turn. After several stories, we understand what the outcome is going to be, and even if we try to play against that outcome, we cannot. Gus is going to die. All the Finch characters are going to die. Barthes would call this a readerly text because of the constraints of its narrative form. We must play our role in each character's death, and it is intentionally heartbreaking. The creative director of the game, Ian Dallas, is an avid student of literature and has designed both the narrative and interactive elements of the game to work together to produce a literary and performative experience for players. Dallas cites authors such as H. P. Lovecraft, Neil Gaiman, Edgar Allan Poe, and Gabriel Garcia Márquez as primary inspirations for the game (Matulef 2017). Among those inspirations are authors that often use literary techniques such as magic realism and the objective correlative. *Magic realism* often takes place in a recognizable, everyday setting, like the wedding in Gus's story, but introduces extraordinary and inexplicable events or elements without explanation, treating them as a normal part of the narrative. In the game, Gus's kite at first seems to be a real everyday object, but when it begins to pick up items from the party and toss them around the sky, the player realizes that we're not dealing with reality anymore. The line is blurred between the mundane and the fantastical, creating a sense of wonder and ambiguity. How could the kite have picked up all those objects? Was the entire story all a symbolic metaphor for Gus being picked up in a storm of emotion, tossed around the sky, only to be blown away and later found on the rocks near the seawater?

The storm in Gus's story is an example of an *objective correlative*, a literary device where the emotions of the scene are externalized, often in weather or objects that reflect the character's internal emotions (see figure 4.3). In an essay referencing Shakespeare's *Hamlet,* poet T. S. Eliot (1932) defines an objective correlative as "a set of objects, a situation, a chain of events which shall be the formula of that *particular* emotion" that the poet feels and hopes to evoke in the reader (para. 11). Storms are the most typical form of objective correlative—almost stereotypical—and yet, in the instance of Gus's story, they are beautifully poetic. Like the kite line and Dawn's poem wrapped around the spool, was Gus also unraveling? Was he windswept in emotions just as the words, chairs, and other objects had become? Although the outcome was foreshadowed (another literary device) and the episode has a predetermined outcome, it still invited exploration of the boundaries of the possible and the impossible through play as performance and interpretation of Dawn's poem with ambiguous meaning. As a result, Farber came away with an increased sense of wonder about the world of the Finches.

But Farber didn't just arrive at this aesthetic experience directly. First, he played efferently, learning how to control the kite, swaying

Figure 4.3
Magic realism and the objective correlative as players fly Gus's kite into the storm in *What Remains of Edith Finch.*

left and right, observing how the words of the poem could be caught. Once he understood the fairly simple controls, he could turn his attention to the more ambiguous beats of the scene and the anticipation of its inevitable conclusion. Farber also replayed this scene several times, not to "win" by catching more objects quicker, but to gain a deeper understanding of meaning. Literature professor David Greenham (2019) describes this act of rereading an experience as essential to the process of close reading, as a first reading can be "transitory"—a brief, if not somewhat fleeting, interlude with text (29). Through rereading the scene by replaying it, Farber began to "possess" the author's ideas (Greenham 2019, 30). As noted, this may be considered readerly in the sense that this game has a strong authorial intent to its narrative and does not allow players to deviate from its inevitable course, but within the course of that story, players, including Farber, report strong aesthetic responses to the experience. Some players even feel triggered by the deaths of the characters.

When Fullerton played the game, she could not complete one of the other levels for some time. The story of baby Gregory, who is playing in the bathtub while his parents fight, is a particularly difficult scene for many players. In the scene, we can play with the toys in the bathtub, bouncing a frog higher and higher, filled with the joy of Gregory's imagination. His mother, Kay, is nearby but on the telephone arguing with Sam, his father. When we see the danger, how Gregory's play is going to knock open the tap and let in too much water, it is almost too late to stop the tragedy. What will happen to the baby when the water level inevitably rises? When Fullerton played, she tried not to complete the game's objective, trying to keep Gregory alive as long as possible, but the only way not to perform as Gregory was to quit playing entirely. Such was the nature of the role-playing in this game: we must take on the role of an innocent child whose gleeful play is going to doom him to drowning. What if we refused to playact in order to try to save Gregory or even Gus?

Refusing invitations to be a performer reduces a game like *Edith Finch* to its puzzle-based mechanics. Players could simply focus on completing levels rather than acting in the scenes, speedrunning to "win" or "beat" each scene by racing to the end. Players could similarly tune out Dawn's poem or the voice-over of Gregory's father, Sam, just going through the efferent motions of flying Gus's kite or bouncing Gregory's frog as quickly as possible. In practice, speeding up our play, diminishing our emotional relationship to the experience, also means quickening the demise of Finch characters. This can be especially heartbreaking when we consider how dramatic elements interplay with the game's formal elements. We simply cannot get anything out of this game without slowing down, performing as the characters, and participating in the evolving tragedy of their collective lives. In this way, like our initial discussion of *Unpacking*, *Edith Finch* is a game that makes little sense if we try to play it from a completely efferent stance. We must become performers, and we must become readers of the aesthetic aspects of these texts to appreciate their full potential.

Farber shared his experience of playing *Edith Finch* with Fullerton, who had also played and "read" the game. She brought up Eliot's (1919) concept of the objective correlative, helping Farber to gain a deeper appreciation of the thematic elements of the game as a complex text. He also thought of a section of Christopher Vogler's (1992) *The Writer's Journey*, where Dorothy Gale's tornadic adventure into the "special world" of Oz in the film *The Wizard of Oz* (Fleming 1939) is foreshadowed through the language of symbolism at the Gale family farm. A gale, of course, is also a strong wind. Dorothy, like Gus, had a storm brewing inside her.

Discussing how the events of the games we were sharing in this chapter all contained literary techniques to cue the players' performances, Fullerton brought up the fact that in *Before the Storm* the raging fire that kept the actress playing Ariel from making it to the theater on time was started by Rachel and Chloe in Episode One of that game. That fire raging throughout the game episodes is an objective correlative with the girls' relationship. Its smoke fills the sky at key moments, and its flames threaten to destroy them in the end. This kind of discussion and mutual unpacking of each other's game experiences is something we return to in chapter 8 as we talk about how we become better readers of games when engaged in a community of readers. As both Rosenblatt's and Dewey's writings show, the activity of forming meaning around our aesthetic experiences is most powerful when performed in a social setting, a community in which the "work" of art is to engage in dialogue around it (Faust 2000, 15).

More and more, as we see games written by narrative designers who understand classic literary techniques, including these kinds of literary structures, we wonder if the potential for play as performance will grow as well, leading to a kind of expectation on the part of players that they will want and need to take on the motivations of player characters and the difficult challenges of their stories. Echoing both Brenda Laurel's (1993) and Janet Murray's (1997) foundational discussions in *Computers as Theater* and *Hamlet on the Holodeck*, we imagine the possibilities of games that are like *Star Trek*'s holodeck experiences: where players role-play in deeply immersive situations with characters who are richly imagined and whose stories push the boundaries of what we think of as "play," to become "playacting." In this kind of play, player character motivation would necessarily go beyond Upton's (2018) ideas of anticipatory play, which describe the machinations in players' minds about uncertainties of what may or may not happen next before an action is taken in a game, or which describe even the ambiguity of narrative beats, which again, focuses on the player's wondering about what may occur. More than an anticipation of outcomes, character motivation considers narrative contexts that inform the intent of our play. It is the "why" of a character's actions. Or as actors famously ask, "What's my motivation for this scene?" Different from motivational theories commonly applied to video games, like extrinsic and intrinsic goal-setting, character motivation is about the performer's understanding of their character's intent. At the level of performance play we are considering, character motivation is crucial to a player's ability to experience a scene aesthetically and to act in that scene accordingly. For example, in role-playing games, this can lead to a phenomenon known as *bleed*, "in which the feelings, thoughts, relationships, and physical states of the player affect the character and vice versa" (Bowman 2018, 385). Bleed has been observed in LARPs and tabletop role-playing games, when players' personalities and emotions begin to "spillover" or bleed into the characters they inhabit (Beltrán 2012, as cited in Bowman 2015, para. 11).

Narrative game writers often share about how they create backstories that set up a character's motivation. In the case of *Before the Storm*, the game codirector Chris Floyd shared with Fullerton how the team thought about the motivations of the player as aligned with the character of Chloe. In the first episode, the team planned to stage an emotional conversation between Rachel and Chloe in a junkyard. Originally, the scene started with the player character trying to cheer up Rachel by smashing junk with a baseball bat for fun. The scene ended with her friend rejecting the overtures and leaving the player character alone in the junkyard. Floyd told Fullerton, "The smashing gameplay, though, lacked the clear player goals we normally aimed for, and emotionally, we feared the player would feel like they failed at the end of it, despite doing what we asked them to do." In the end, the team realized that they needed to motivate the smashing gameplay for the player more clearly. So they turned the character conversation into a kind of breakup scene, where Rachel, upset for a different reason, tells Chloe, "I can't be your friend right now." After she leaves, the player, as Chloe, is motivated to take out their hurt at the "breakup" on the objects in the junkyard, each of which represents a frustration in the character's life—family, school, and her new friend are all smashed with abandon as we take on Chloe's pain and work through it as a dramatic performance of that pain.

When Fullerton played as Chloe, she found the smashing scene freeing and cathartic until its final moments when Chloe comes face to face with a broken wreck of a car—reminding the character of her father's car, which he crashed and died in. The underlying motivation for all of Chloe's anguish was revealed to the player at a critical moment, and the surprising pain of it was real to Fullerton as a player. Similarly, when Farber played *Edith Finch* as Gus, he channeled feelings of exasperation and anger into his performance of Gus's story. And, when he played as a cat in *Stray*, he considered the virtual physicality each scene demanded as he made catlike leaps onto platforms or took time to cuddle up next to robots, conveying warmth. These kinds of moments, where the player has been motivated by the game to care about why something is happening, are the moments in which aesthetic readings and performances take flight. When players call on their own personal experiences in response to situations in the same way an actor would in a theatrical play, they find their emotions linked inextricably to those of a character. Playing through those emotions gives rise to the real potential of play as performance: not banal choices between equipping a character with this item or that, or choosing one hairstyle over another, but deeply motivated actions that bind us to a character's fate and help us to evoke our own performance of that fate and our own reading of why it happens the way that it does.

Let's conclude this discussion of performative play by looking at a reading of another game in the *Life Is Strange* series: *Life Is Strange 2* (DON'T NOD 2018). The game, as with *Before the Storm*, is divided into episodes, with language that explicitly invites players to perform their parts. It follows the story of two brothers, Sean and Daniel Diaz, which begins in a small town near Seattle. Its environmental storytelling is similar to immersive theater, as players are invited to interact with scenic elements, dialogue, and open-ended outcomes that require interpretation. In the opening scenes, a supernatural incident leads to a tragedy that sets the narrative in motion. Fearing the consequences of this tragedy, Sean and Daniel embark on a journey to Mexico, their father's homeland. The central gameplay involves player choices that affect the narrative and relationships between characters, which can lead to seven possible endings. Although there are finite decisions that can be made, players are sometimes afforded unlimited time to linger, ruminate, and process parts of the narrative in interludes similar to those described in chapter 3. Throughout the journey, Sean and Daniel encounter both kindness and hostility from the people they meet, highlighting themes of prejudice, family bonds, and personal growth. The gameplay presents the harsh realities of modern America around social and political issues such as immigration and racism, illuminating how these topics affect the characters' lives.

In a pivotal scene, the brothers, hungry and tired from their time on the road, encounter a gas station where they hope to get food and supplies. But they don't have much money, so their options are limited. When Fullerton played as older brother Sean, she journaled:

> As I walk up to the station, I see a white family eating lunch at a picnic table outside. A chubby mom, a dad, and a girl. They all seem to be studiously avoiding my eyes. I feel self-conscious as Daniel, and I approach. The conversation is really awkward. I can tell what they think: here are two beggars looking for money. I try my best to seem "normal," but I can tell they aren't buying it. We talk a bit, but the dad gets grumpy and tells me I'm interrupting their "family time." When I finally ask if they could spare some food, they refuse. The little girl even laughs at us. I'm humiliated. I decide to go clean up in the bathroom before going into the gas station, hoping for better luck. Sean is covered in blood from the accident. We're so alone. Something about the quiet privacy of the bathroom reminds me of why we're here. Dad is dead. We're all alone. I'm in charge. But I'm just a kid, and Daniel's really a kid. How can I keep him safe? Finally, I lead us out of the bathroom, and we go into the gas station

> store. Inside, Daniel is excited about everything—candy, playing games, all the things we can't afford. The store clerk is doing a crossword puzzle and not paying much attention to us. As I browse, I realize that I have the option to buy a lot of things: camping equipment, food, trail maps, and so on. Or . . . I can steal some of these things (see figure 4.4). While I consider this option, Daniel finds a puppy and falls in love with it. I have to tell him we can't have it, even though I want it too. I have to play the adult now. He accepts the no, thankfully, and turns his attention to a creepy-looking guy sitting in the café area looking at questionable internet sites on his laptop. Daniel talks to the man as I turn back to the food and think again about stealing it. No, I can't do that. Can I? If I steal something, aren't I just fulfilling the expectations of those prejudiced people outside? I'm torn between taking care of Daniel by stealing food for us and staying honest, which I really want to do. I decide to buy a Chocobar for Daniel, the honest way. I'm not reduced to stealing—yet.

As we can see, this scene is set up to ask us to perform as we think Sean should—but we're not told exactly what that means. Sean, as a character, has conflicting motivations, so the scene has a multitude of dramatic possibilities. Maybe the shopkeeper will take pity on us and let us buy more than we have money for? Or maybe the creepy

Figure 4.4
Sean considers stealing from the store in *Life Is Strange 2*.

guy will give us some money? Do we need to get a sleeping bag, or will we find a place to sleep inside tonight? We just don't know what to expect, and this heightens the ambiguity of the narrative choices. There is also the specter of racial prejudice we experienced from the family at the table. Will we get similar treatment from the shopkeeper or the creepy guy? Fullerton journaled:

> It's a lot to consider, and I spend a lot of time wandering around the store, uncertain what to do. Finally, I buy some water and hotdogs along with the Chocobar. Keeping as much money as possible for whatever comes down the road. I take a free map and we go outside to eat. As we look at the map, a big white man with a beard comes up suddenly and accuses us of stealing the food. I have to decide how to handle it, and I try to talk to him reasonably rather than fight or flee, but it doesn't matter. He tries to drag us inside and the scene gets out of control fast. Suddenly, I'm knocked unconscious and it's my worst nightmare. We're caught up in what feels like another horrible situation in an America that isn't kind to people like me and Daniel.

As can be gathered from this scene, even a game that is a "readerly text" or one that we think of as "on rails" can have deep and conflicting opportunities for players to engage in character motivations and complicated performances. Although the gas station scene will always end in an altercation, the choices we make and why we make them here are central to our performance as Sean and, ultimately, to the role model we provide for Daniel. That role model will change how Daniel acts and how he turns out in this story, which has several very different outcomes. We cannot play this scene to "win" it in any conventional game sense. We cannot speed through it, efferently, choosing exactly the "right" items from the store. We can only live it, as Sean and Daniel do, and consider the meaning of our actions in the context of this hostile America, and wonder what will be the outcome of our performance. When we have lived an experience like this, one that is complicated emotionally and morally, we need to reflect on it after the fact, unpack the moments beat by beat to understand why it happened the way that it did and how our reading of the situation was colored by our own personal baggage. What did we bring to our part in this play? And what kind of reading did our interpretation of the role evoke?

In many ways, the performative experiences described here are clearly an extension of the similar experiences we have when we project our own hopes and fears onto experiences in any media or form. When we read or watch a play like *Romeo and Juliet,* we pray that the lovers' messages will reach each other in time to stop the inevitable tragedy—even if we have experienced the play before and know how it ends. Our emotions are invested in the characters' plight even if, or perhaps especially if, we know what is to come. We hold our breath in some faint hope things will work out differently this time. As with the reading of *Life Is Strange 2* described by Fullerton above, even when she deliberately chooses to play Sean true to his morals, the tragedy of prejudice and violence will still play out. It is the reading of that experience that will be different for each player. Had Fullerton chosen to make Sean steal from the store, one might read the beating that happens afterward somewhat differently. In fact, some players might go into the store with the objective of stealing as much as possible, ignoring the moral question entirely. In this case, the violent response at the end of the scene could feel somewhat justified, preparing the player for the depiction of a much more hardened worldview. Clearly, the responses we have when we read, watch, or perform experiences like these are not based on whether that experience is written, visualized, played, or performed. Rather, they are related to the alignment of our motivations with those of the characters, to the personal "baggage" we bring to each evocation of a text, and to the process of reflecting on those experiences during and after the fact, which we discuss at length in the next chapter.

5
Reflecting on Gameplay

In game designer Greg Trefry's essay in the book *Well Played 3.0* (Davidson 2011), he reflects on playing a live-action street game, *La Noche de los Muertos* (Johnson, Reddington, and Grian 2009), that took place in the city of Bristol, England. He describes his deep play experience in a breathless, fear-soaked narrative. Trefry (2011) writes, "My feet pound the street in time with my racing heart. I reach the end of the bridge and bolt left down the street running parallel to the river. My lungs burn from the dash. I'm not sure I can keep going. I sprint out of the glow of the streetlight and behind a shed implanted in the center of a small parking lot. I glance back over my shoulder to see if anyone's following me. No one is" (237).

Trefry is playing the part of a masked survivor, avoiding the undead while collecting trophies at a series of tombs, crypts, and memorial checkpoints. His team must try to stay together while being chased by undead zombies and hooded figures. At one point, the team is so scared they each run their own way. "I think about my reaction and my unwillingness to sacrifice myself for a teammate," Trefry (2011) muses. "I ask myself, what should I have done? Some part of me thinks the noble act would have been to try and save my teammates. But what could I have done other than run?" (244).

Trefry's moral musings are interesting and bring his writing alive as they prompt his readers to wonder if they, too, would have run. Or would they have sacrificed themselves? Would they have stuck together with their team for mutual safety or mutual demise? But almost immediately after his fascinating deliberation, Trefry begins to fear that he is "simply recounting stories about [his] personal experience of the game," as if this were a bad thing or something less important and not scholarly (246). He recalls the game designer Nick Fortugno telling him a theory of why games and narrative are often mismatched. Fortugno, as per Trefry, says, "Games are like dance. They are about the experience you have while playing. That experience can be powerful and even take on a sense of connection and narrative for the dancer. You experience it and build a narrative in your head out of all your moves. But describing it often just comes across as a series of mundane choices. I tend to agree with him" (246).

Fortugno and Trefry aren't precisely wrong: listening to a player relate a list of mundane choices *is* boring. But this isn't what encompasses a player's experience, and unless they are tremendously bad storytellers, why would they describe it as such after having a rich and meaningful experience? Trefry himself describes his own play with passion and immediacy. So, too, have the several other Well Played essays we've quoted. Our own personal readings of games are full of emotional details and engaging moments of anticipation, fear, wonder, excitement, joy, surprise, sacrifice, tenderness, and more. It's true, though: some people are just good storytellers, and some people are not. Some people can tell you a rip-roaring tale of going to the podiatrist. Some people can make an epic adventure boring and tedious. The fault is not in the aesthetic form of games: it lies in the skill of distilling, reflecting, and finding meaning in our own play. We might all tell wonderful stories about experiences that we have—if we are able to reflect meaningfully on them, speak or write articulately about them, and connect them to the universal themes of our lives and world. In this way, games are no different from other experiences we have, even if our expectations of them have not driven us yet to learn these skills. But if this art form is to be, as so many have claimed, the most important medium of this century, then some of us must learn to be better players and to bring back from the land of play our epic stories of games well-played.

We need to become better readers of games, better performers of play, and better able to capture and reflect upon just what it is that happens to us inside the world of a game so that we can bring that reflection back with us to the world outside the game. As we see in this chapter, the ability to reflect on our play and to use that reflection to transform our understanding of our lives outside the game holds a promise for how powerful that play can be—for us as individuals and in our wider communities. The ability to take on new roles and perspectives in play and to reflect on the experiences we have from those perspectives can broaden our understanding of the lives of others and, by extension, harking back to Rosenblatt and Dewey, help us to negotiate a more plural and democratic society.

As mentioned in chapter 4, the notion of the magic circle is that it bounds our play and offers permission and license to act according to the rules of play rather than the rules of living. In 1990, Rudine Sims Bishop proposed a related metaphor for the liminal boundaries of books. Her influential essay "Mirrors, Windows, and Sliding Glass Doors" describes the way in which we, when we read, see ourselves reflected in the characters and worlds of books and immersed in their narratives. Bishop (1990) wrote, "Books are sometimes windows, offering views of worlds that may be real or imagined, familiar or strange. These windows are also sliding glass doors, and readers have only to walk through in imagination to become part of whatever world has been created or recreated by the author. When lighting conditions are just right, however, a window can also be a mirror" (ix).

These similar metaphors for understanding how we can see ourselves simultaneously protected and challenged, reflected and transported in the imaginative worlds of fictional and playful media, are the foundation of what we explore here as "reflective play." For many years, Fullerton has spoken about this concept of reflective play in talks about games made in her research center at the University of Southern California (USC) Game Innovation Lab, including *Cloud* (Jenova Chen 2006), *The Night Journey*, and *Walden, a game*. In her 2017 keynote talk at Games for Change, Fullerton defined a concept of reflective play, stating, "By this, I mean play that allows for, and even depends upon, an internal and emotional process on the part of players—play that nurtures that internal process through its design, its scope, and its pace. . . . My interest in this kind of slow-paced play is not because slowness itself is equivalent to meaningfulness but rather because the process of making meaning through reflection requires time at a human pace, takes cycles of response, interpretation, and unpacking of experience" (Fullerton 2017, 9:25).

This notion that reflective play is an internal and emotional process on the part of players is echoed in Upton's (2017) guiding principle of situational design, which he says is "to focus on what the player believes about the game rather than the game itself" (82). Upton goes on to discuss the way in which players understand the meaning of games as what he calls the "residue of experience" (112). "In a narrow technical sense," he continues, "all games are meaningful because all games encourage us to develop strategies to help us play them. However, the meanings we take away from many games are self-referential." But what about games that we have played closely and deeply and which leave us with what Upton calls "a lingering emotional resonance" (112)? Or what Fullerton (2017) calls "games that emphasize the varied human experience of players, rather than focusing on the way in which they manipulate the game . . . games which attempt to provoke, and respect, the inner life of player, which strive to create a playful space in which to reflect on the ongoing narratives that we are all so busy creating as we engage with life" (5:53)?

Upton (2017) gives an example of this type of reflective play in the cooperative game *Journey* (thatgamecompany 2012), in which players, in the role of abstract pilgrims, face a lonely journey across a barren vista—until they are randomly assigned a partner, another pilgrim, who joins them on their trek. He describes the way in which players learn, through play, not exposition, that the closer you stay to your partner, the faster your ability to "glide" over obstacles will recharge. One of the "meanings" of *Journey*, he concludes, is "the sense that on a hard journey, we're better off if we stick together. The game doesn't tell us this. It invites us to perform it" (115). Upton describes how, if we want to learn something such as this message that *Journey* has to tell us, we need time for introspection. When something significant happens, we need space and stillness—both in the game and after the game—to think about what unfolded and what it means. We can see this clearly in the

Figure 5.1
Playing with a partner in *Journey*.

player quotation that opened the introduction of this book, where, in the weeks after her father's death, fifteen-year-old Sophia Ouellette reflects on her experiences playing *Journey* with her father and realizes how the memory of their playthrough has given her a sense of solace about the bittersweet nature of the end of life.

As Fullerton played the final version of *Journey* for the first time, she also had an experience that exemplifies the internal emotional process of players making meaning through reflective play. *Journey* is a unique type of multiplayer game in that you cannot know who your play companions are until the end of the game. Even with this kind of anonymity, players tend to form strong bonds with their coplayers, as seen in this description. Fullerton journaled:

> I am traveling with my randomly assigned companion. We have gotten really good at flying together to charge each other up. We are flying, almost dancing and "pinging" at each other joyfully as we make our way through the game. Then we come to a bridge, and suddenly, without warning, my companion falls off. It is so unexpected; I hardly know what to do. I try to see where they have fallen, to see if I can help them back up. But I cannot see them. I wait . . . to see if they will respawn near me, but they don't. I run back and forth on the bridge, "pinging" over and over in case they can hear me. It is an existential cry into the void below the bridge. I don't know who they are because your partner in the game is assigned to you randomly and is nameless until the end. So, I have no way to contact them outside the game. I feel that I cannot leave this spot, though. Would I leave a friend if we had been separated like this on a real-world journey? Never, never! I run back and forth, crying out, "ping, ping, ping!" My lament echoes in the absolute loneliness of the game I am now faced with finishing alone. I don't know how long I wait, but finally, reluctantly, I turn and make my way across the bridge. I continue my journey alone (see figure 5.2). But part of my heart is still on that bridge. To this day, I wonder what became of them, if they knew the agony I was in when they fell. It was a rehearsal for the kind of anguish we feel when we lose a friend suddenly along our way in life. I don't mean to say it was the same as that kind of grief and anguish, but in some ways, it was a reflection of that kind of experience before I had actually felt it.

Figure 5.2
Continuing across the bridge alone in *Journey*.

Bishop's (1990) concept of mirrors is evocative because she qualifies her metaphor to say that the "lighting conditions" must be "just right" to make us see ourselves reflected back in books that we read. This is because, though we are always looking for ourselves in books, trying to make personal connections, we don't always find characters or situations that we deeply relate to. This may be because the book is about a character who is very different from us or whose culture we are not familiar with. In this case, the book might provide a window or a sliding door to view or enter a world that is not our own. Windows and sliding doors are wonderful ways to learn and grow—we learn to empathize with characters who are not like us, and we come to understand more about those characters' worlds and cultures. We can still make connections and still find ourselves mirrored in parts of their journey—reading about an alien who gets bullied in a faraway galaxy can be a window into different experiences or a mirror of a reader's lived experience. A sliding door is a way that a book gives entry into an entire world or culture. We may meet characters who speak in a vernacular different from ours and begin to understand a wider breadth of experiences by following their journeys. In this way, Bishop (1990) writes, "Literature transforms human experience and reflects it back to us, and in that reflection, we can see our own lives and experiences as part of the larger human experience. Reading, then, becomes a means of self-affirmation, and readers often seek their mirrors in books" (ix).

Games, too, in some of the same ways as literature, can function as mirrors, windows, and sliding doors. The lived experience of a player, when activated by a deeply felt moment of gameplay or narrative, can provoke players to reflect on their own identity or life, and see it, as Bishop writes of readers, as part of the larger human experience. The way in which games provoke such experiences is related to literature but also to the aural and visual languages of cinema, painting, music, and theater.

We have been using the word "reading" to describe the way in which players make meaning within games, but, as we have said, that is not meant to constrain us to textual experiences. As Gee (2007) observes, "Gamers, of course, decode and comprehend ('consume') game design when they react effectively to that design in order to play the game. However, that game design doesn't really come into full existence until players make decisions and take actions in the game (otherwise the first screen of the game just sits there)" (135). Active viewers read the visual languages of painting and cinema, just as active listeners read the aural language of music and theater. We can certainly find our emotions reflected in the passionate score of a film or the deep shadows of a painting. Just as a viewer of *The Godfather* (Coppola 1972) watches, enrapt, as Michael Corleone moves from the bright, sunny lighting of his sister's wedding in the opening scenes of the film to the dark shadows of his father's study in its final moments, having taken the downward spiral into his family's dark business, so, too, do we play through the visual and audio transitions of a game like *Journey*, reading its multimodal storytelling languages much as we would a cinematic experience.

In film professor Bruce Block's (2008) foundational text on cinematic storytelling, *The Visual Story*, he breaks down the way in which each graphic component of visual storytelling can be designed and controlled by the filmmaker to convey meaning and underscore thematic intentions. Techniques such as the manipulation of contrast and affinity of visual elements to increase or decrease conflict in the arc of experience are a key focus of the book. Color, for example, can be used throughout a visual story to denote a particular emotion or idea. In the example from *The Godfather*, the tone of the lighting—bright and flat versus dark and shadowy—changes over the course of the story to visually reflect Michael's moral descent, his journey into darkness.

In *Journey*, Jenova Chen, who studied under Bruce Block at USC, uses similar techniques to evoke a sense of emotional change over the course of the game. In the early levels, the world is monochromatic: a sea of sand in beige and brown. As the player moves to the middle levels, the world shifts gradually and then suddenly, creating several moments of strong visual contrast. As Fullerton wrote when she played,

> I come upon a large, corroding structure in the sands, and as I move through it, the camera, which has been free until now, is constrained to the side, flattening my view to a limited perspective as columns fly by as I glide past them, giving a sense of almost uncontrolled speed through the structure (see figure 5.3). The sun is setting; it glints on the sand, creating bright highlights and deep shadows. Even as I am constrained in this view, it is electric and visually stunning. I have not seen this world so full of such sharp lines and contrast before, and the shift makes me take a breath and hold it. Then it is over, and I am skiing down a slope; the camera is free again, and I can move from side to side as I slide, or ski, as it feels like I am doing. The dark contrast of the late afternoon sun makes it exciting and difficult to navigate. The music is wild, with pizzicato strings matching the energy of the visuals. As I reach the end of the passage, the contrast growing as the sun sets, I ski off a ledge, hang, and fall . . . fall into darkness, into silence, into deep,

Figure 5.3
Contrast creating emotion in *Journey*.

> deep blue, into the abyss. I am both thrilled and afraid. I am alone, having lost my companion, and I wonder if I'll be able to make it through the abyss without a partner, as I know it is meant to be faced by two players working together. Ahead of me, a huge monster rears its head. There's no time to wonder, I have to act quickly.

The color of the next, lower level, which the player falls into after this scene, is meant to represent the "abyss" of the hero's journey that forms the underlying structure of the game. The hero's journey is, of course, a well-explored narrative structure across many forms of storytelling, with its main goal to dramatize for us how a naive hero can take on the challenges of a world of adventure, facing trials, gaining allies and mentors, learning and growing through the worst of these until they come through the abyss, claim the "elixir" or the reward they were seeking, and return to the ordinary world, changed forever. As we see in this scene from *Journey*, the trials that characters face as part of the hero's journey are meant to challenge our sense of self, our abilities, and our commitment to the goals we are seeking. The hero's journey is meant to change us and send us back to the world with new knowledge, a new perspective, and the skills and experience we lacked beforehand. This archetypal story structure, identified by literature professor Joseph Campbell (1949) through his work in comparative mythology and religion, does not map to every story, hero, or heroine, of course, but it is quite often taught in literature, film, and creative writing classes—and, importantly, now in game design classes. It has influenced the thinking of many storytellers through the success of filmmaker George Lucas's adherence to its structure in his classic *Star Wars* films and the influential text *The Writer's Journey* by Christopher Vogler (1992). There may be no better example of a naive hero than the character of Luke Skywalker in the original *Star Wars* (Lucas 1977), nor a clearer visual example of the "call to adventure" than Princess Leia's holographic plea, "Help me, Obi-Wan Kenobi, you're my only hope."

Similarly, the hero's journey is often taken as a model for game narratives like *Journey*. Jenova Chen carefully mapped the dramatic beats to give his abstract pilgrimage a strong emotional arc. In terms of reflective play, however, the importance of the hero's journey for viewers and players lies not in knowing or being able to follow the specifics of a well-known structure but in its ability to model for us the importance of growth, change, and self-reflection as we face our greatest trials. What is important is that, as we view a film or play a game, we feel the kind of emotional growth that is only possible when we, in the mode of a hero, face difficult challenges, take great risks, make sacrifices, form connections with allies, and do what we hope is right rather than what is simple or easy. When we, as a hero in such a game, return to our origins changed by an experience, we gain new perspectives and bring back new ways of seeing ourselves and others. Echoing Rosenblatt's assertion that better readers become better citizens, we find that games, too, can act "as a moral and ethical force, helping readers clarify their values and allowing them to share the values of others"—foundational to a democratic system (Flynn 2007, 67). Thinking back to the scene from *Life Is*

Strange 2, as described in chapter 4, where Sean and Daniel face the kind of microaggressions and scrutiny that make up everyday racism for mixed-race people, we can see our play and performance of these young characters as a play of moral growth. Our choices for them along their journey, those that are heroic and those that are not, allow us to live and play from a different perspective as they navigate the difficult multicultural landscape of the game. Games like *Journey* and *Life Is Strange 2*, in their most meaningful moments along their "hero's journey," allow us the possibility of not only seeing ourselves reflected in such moments but also being transported into a different lived experience, one that can build our understanding beyond the confines of the game.

Flow Versus Reflection

We might assume that all games could be read reflectively, especially those that use mythological references like the hero's journey in their story structures, but the truth is that many games, even those about the journeys of heroes, don't support an intense emotional level of player connection and reflection. Even games that use structural elements of the hero's journey in their narrative arcs, for example, don't always provoke reflection upon important universal themes in those narratives. As with all media, some games are just better at moving us than others, and some games have more to share with us about the human experience than others. This isn't meant to be a pejorative statement; not all games need to be about important universal themes to provide interesting and wonderful play. For example, we can consider a game like *Tetris* (Alexey Pajitnov 1984), which most players would agree is an extremely good game. *Tetris* is a game that can be played very deeply, so deeply that players have claimed to have "*Tetris* dreams" and to see *Tetris* patterns after playing for hours upon hours. Our play of *Tetris* could even be read closely and deeply in the ways we've discussed in chapters 2 and 3. And, of course, *Tetris* exhibits one of the most oft-cited aspects of good gameplay: flow.

Flow is a mental state described by psychologist Mihály Csíkszentmihályi (1990) in which a participant in a game or other difficult task finds themselves fully immersed, energized, involved, and enjoying themselves. It is a common design goal for games to put players into this almost hypnotic state of intertwined challenge and pleasure, and players often look for this kind of state when seeking out their favorite game types. But it is not the only pleasure that games can offer. As we have seen in several readings in this chapter already, there are perhaps deeper and more challenging rewards in games that go beyond flow and instead create reflection. Is it the nature of the game verbs in *Tetris* that makes it lean more toward flow than reflection? We would argue that it is not. A player could map an interesting reading of the experience of a factory worker or menial laborer onto the mechanic of *Tetris*, thinking about the way in which we all sync our movements and thoughts to machines these days. Although it would take a highly attuned reader of games to evoke such a reading while engrossed in the type of flow that *Tetris* strives to create, it is certainly possible. And, when we discuss the literary pleasures of reading games in chapter 7, we see that there are definitely players such as this, who use the flow state that *Tetris* and similar puzzle games create to let their minds muse on the nature of life and responsibility. We also know that there are games that use very similar mechanics but very different dramatic elements to provoke players out of flow and into a state of reflection.

To find a game like this, we need only turn back to *Edith Finch*. In one of the final stories of the Finch family, we meet Lewis, a menial worker in a fish cannery whose life is in a state of despair. In Lewis's story, players take on his rote mechanical task of chopping salmon heads in the cannery. As players slice fish over and over, they start to see a parallel fantasy world overlaid on the chopping block, where

Lewis plays out his dream of being a hero in a fantastical adventure. At first, the fantasy takes up just part of the workspace; soon enough, it grows to cover the screen. In the fantasy world, Lewis goes on a journey not unlike that of the hero's journey while, in a puzzle-like mechanic that echoes a game of *Tetris*, the players slice fish heads. As they do, they experience the deep schism between Lewis's inner world of imagination and his external circumstances. The scene of rote manual labor embodied in the puzzle mechanic is accompanied by a dramatic voice-over as players hear and read a letter written by his psychiatrist, Dr. Emily Nuth, to the Finch family. When Farber played, he wrote the following:

> A dead fish appears on the screen, and with my right-hand thumbstick and buttons on the controller, I move the dead salmon into position and click to slice off its head. Oddly satisfying, I nevertheless understand how Lewis would become quickly bored at this job. As the psychiatrist reads, "His mind began to . . . wander," her tone also seems to wander. A maze appears on the empty half of the cutting board. Her phrase and a wandering character that I can now control with my left thumbstick appear.
>
> I wander the labyrinth with one thumbstick, which grows increasingly more visually compelling—from 2D to 3D—while I slice fish with my other hand. "He knew the world was all in his imagination, but he was so proud of having created it," Dr. Nuth reads. "In his own eyes, he'd become something greater than a king. For someone who'd never known success in the real world, I think it was overwhelming. And then it struck him that the real Lewis was not the one chopping salmon, but the one climbing the steps of a golden palace." I wonder, do I, too, prefer the imaginary world to Lewis's ruthlessly monotonous existence? Is the fantastical hallucination from Lewis's psychosis or his drug abuse?

The fantasy gameplay (see figure 5.4) consumes and overcomes Lewis's reality—and ours, as well—on-screen and metaphorically. By the end of Lewis's story, it becomes apparent his vivid daydreams are a coping mechanism to endure the mundane reality of his life, which he can no longer tolerate. It culminates with players

Figure 5.4
Lewis Finch's fantasy world overtakes his mundane reality in *What Remains of Edith Finch*.

being given a singular choice: to have Lewis bend down his head into a guillotine in order for his imagined self to be crowned king. As mentioned, players hear his psychiatrist, which explicitly invites a psychoanalytical reading. Players may then reflect on Lewis's psychological state, his implied substance abuse, the curse of the Finch family, and, perhaps, their own rote existence.

There is a clear difference between playing *Tetris* and playing this emotionally difficult level of *Edith Finch*. And yet the mechanics themselves are not that different: rotating and moving blocks as they drop versus sorting and chopping fish as they drop. But *Tetris* intends to put us in a state of flow, whereas *Edith Finch* invites us into a state of reflection. Again, this is not to say that one type of play should be valued above the other. Instead, we are saying that in a game like *Edith Finch*, which takes much of its design aesthetics from the literary genre of the family history, there is a clear intention to provoke reflective play; in *Tetris*, there is a clear intention to absorb the player into a state that blocks extraneous thoughts.

It's interesting to note that as we have moved our focus from a close and deep reading of more formal systems of play to the more performative and dramatic aspects of play, we have also moved from discussing platforming and puzzling to performance and narrative play mechanics. As with games that signal the player to perform, there also seem to be games that signal the player to reflect on their play. For example, we can look at slow-paced, open texts like *That Dragon, Cancer* (Numinous Games 2016), a deeply emotional and autobiographical video game that revolves around the real-life experiences of Joel Green, a young boy diagnosed with terminal cancer, and his family. *That Dragon, Cancer* does not use puzzle mechanics or attempt to build flow for players. Instead, the game uses activity-focused minigames in each scene, sometimes calling the player's attention to the kind of daily minutiae that make up the life experiences of the Green family as they deal with Joel's treatments. In one scene, an inconsolable and ill Joel is in his hospital bed. Joel's crying cannot be quieted by any player interaction. Offers of juice, songs, and cradles are turned away. Agency here is intentionally restricted, forcing failure and messaging hopelessness (Farber and Schrier 2021). When Farber first played *That Dragon, Cancer*, he reflected on his son, who was the same age as Joel at the time. He thought about past feelings of powerlessness in fatherhood and, more broadly, in life. He also thought about free will and the human condition. These are heavy ideas to play with on and off the screen. Fullerton, who was going through cancer treatment herself when the game was released, could not bring herself to play it until several years later. When she finally did play it, she experienced a deep sense of resonance with both Joel, as the young patient, and his parents, journaling about that same scene:

> I'm lying on the hospital bed, cradling Joel after hours of crying (see figure 5.5). He is finally asleep. Balloons made of hospital gloves float softly above us like ghost hands. I click on them, tapping them softly back up on the air so they don't fall on Joel and wake him. I

Figure 5.5
Holding baby Joel in the hospital in *That Dragon, Cancer*.

> realize I'm holding my breath in real life, as if I could wake him by breathing. I let the breath slowly out, like I did when I was waiting for the chemo to drip into my own veins. I wonder what it must be like for an infant to go through that. Even as an adult, knowing what was going on, I wanted to cry. Sometimes I did, quietly, silently cry while the toxic chemicals dripped slowly and surely into my arm. I realize I can stroke the baby in his sleep, and I do it carefully. As I lie there, my eyes begin to droop closed. The screen dips to black quickly several times, and I realize the moment of peace is coming to a close. What will come next? I don't know, I can only live in this moment with the child in my arms and the memories filling my mind. My eyes finally close as the screen falls dark.

We can think back to Upton's description of anticipatory play, described in chapter 3, when we read an entry like this and understand what he means when he says that it "takes time" and "requires stillness." Reflection, like anticipation, does take time and can occur in stages, as discussed in social scientist Donald A. Schön's book *The Reflective Practitioner: How Professionals Think in Action* (1983). Players are not professionals, obviously, but they are practitioners nonetheless, people who base their choices on evaluating their actions. Schön describes two different stages of reflection that we can go through. First is *reflection-in-action,* describing when we pause to think about unexpected outcomes in the moment, as ideas are experimented and pivoted, as put into practice in real time, and second is *reflection-on-action,* which occurs after an experience has already taken place. In games, the player may use both of these types of reflection strategically, as in Gee's (2003, 2007) discussion of "good" video games for learning, where players exercise metacognition by reflecting and hypothesizing how a designer might think, which can inform the solutions players test next. However, as we have seen in the readings from *That Dragon, Cancer* and *Life Is Strange 2,* players may also use in-action and on-action reflection to understand the emotional meanings of gameplay activities and events.

There are a number of other games in this kind of slow-paced, exploratory, or interactive narrative genre that rely on deep and reflective play to create meaning. Games like *Gone Home,* discussed in chapter 3, or *Dear Esther* (The Chinese Room 2012), are examples of such games, which have only minimal player mechanics but rely on environmental storytelling, narrative objects, and voice-overs to create a sense of unfolding narrative play. As mentioned in chapter 1, these kinds of games require players to come to the experience prepared to involve themselves in reading their play. If they are not prepared to play aesthetically—to fill in the gaps or ellipses—they will find little to engage them and this has caused quite a lot of misunderstanding from more traditional game players. Here are just a few random comments from internet players of *Gone Home* who clearly do not reflect on their experiences: "There is no gameplay, you just wander a house and read diaries and reveal a couple hidden rooms. Then the game ends" (GameFAQs 2015). "It is slow, but only 2 hours long . . . a 2 hours you will spend waiting for the game to start getting good. It does not" (GameFAQs 2015). Players such as these, who are not willing to approach games with an aesthetic stance, find nothing to "do" in games such as these. They are not putting in effort to fill in narrative gaps in the way that they might engage with strategic moves or puzzles. Such players seem unable to bring a reflective stance to their play, trying to play them efferently and because there is little to do beyond reflect, they find the entire experience lacking. The opportunity for taking a reflective stance can be found beyond the extremes of genres like walking simulators, however, and players who miss the cues to play reflectively in a game like *Gone Home*, may yet pick up on these cues in a game like *Braid*, as discussed in chapter 2, or what we might call a "reflective platformer" like *Gris* (Nomada Studios 2018). *Gris* is a puzzle-platforming game, but one with a richly imagined metaphor that, though it could be played efferently, cannot really be appreciated without reflection on its themes. Fullerton played *Gris* and wrote the following:

> In the opening sequence, I see a young woman sleeping in the palm of a giant, cracked stone hand. She wakes and sings out the notes of a song. But suddenly, tremors in the hand cause it to crack even more. Her voice falters, and she is no longer able to sing. As the stone of the hand crumbles and breaks apart, she falls, tumbling head over heels through clouds, until she lands, collapsed in a heap on the ground. The world, which had been filled with reds, pinks, blues, and pastel yellows, is now black and white, except for her hair, which is green. Her dress, which was red and voluminous, is now black and gray, hanging limply over her hunched body. Now I have control. I use the thumbsticks to try and move her to the right, but she stumbles and falls. Surprised, I try again. Again, she stumbles and falls. This is unexpected in a platform game, and between the opening events and this interactive event, I know that something is dreadfully wrong with this character. She has lost her voice and her will, and even with my participation, she finds it hard to go on (see figure 5.6). I try one more time. This time, I get her to walk slowly, depressively, literally depicted in a fog, barely visible, until she falls again. Again, she gets up, and this time she gazes at the sky for a moment, straightens her shoulders, and, as a bit of music comes in,

Figure 5.6
The protagonist stumbles in the opening of *Gris*.

> I am finally able to run and jump as I originally expected. Playing this sequence is like reading Sylvia Plath's (1963) novel *The Bell Jar*; I feel the protagonist's oppressive mental anxiety through the visuals and the gameplay, just as I felt these emotions through Plath's literary descriptions.

As Fullerton plays through *Gris*, she restores the colors of the young protagonist's world, each set of levels bringing a new color into the palette. She also restores the character's memories by collecting mementos that fill the sky with constellations, all while leading her through the stages of grief: shock, denial, anger, bargaining, depression, and acceptance. As she does, the character gains the confidence to brave winds and crush obstacles by becoming "heavy," to double jump, glide, and fly, and finally to sing again. *Gris* is not an example of a game that follows the hero's journey, and yet it is a game that embodies a universal story: how we come to terms with grief, loss, and our own frailty. It is an experience that requires reflection on these themes to make sense, even as it requires puzzle-solving skills to move through its world.

Complicated Emotions and Catharsis

Games like *Tetris* divert us away from real-world issues and everyday problems, and we take joy in rotating tetrominoes as they cascade down, fitting them into tight rows. As already discussed, however,

Tetris, though a wonderful game, does not invite the kind of reflection on its puzzle mechanics that we find in games like *Edith Finch* or *Gris*. Rather, it invites a kind of completionist pleasure, what we can see as a *hedonic* experience (Greek for pleasure); we feel good playing games like *Tetris* because they allow us to reduce our view of the world to an experience that can be controlled, that feels orderly and understandable. Hedonic experiences include many sources of enjoyment that elicit positive, uncomplicated emotions, like some romantic comedies and children's cartoons, and many video games, such as *Mario Kart* (Nintendo 1992–), *Animal Crossing* (Nintendo 2001–), and *Minecraft* (Mojang 2011). So many video games offer uncomplicated pleasures that we often generalize them as escapist media. But as we have seen, there are a growing number of games that offer more complicated experiences for players to reflect on as they play. These games, like *Gris*, *Lost Words*, and the *Life Is Strange* games, offer *eudaimonic* experiences more than hedonic ones. Eudaimonic media engenders a deeper sense of personal growth and well-being. When we watch thought-provoking documentaries and films and read powerful books, we reflect on the more complicated set of emotions they offer, including connections to history, people, and cultures beyond our personal experiences. This kind of enriching experience prompts reflection, intellectual growth, and emotional engagement. Video games, as we've discussed, can provide players with a practice space to learn how to cope with emotions, such as grief and loss, or how to understand the kind of microaggressions faced by those who are different in our society. They can allow us to rehearse our responses to challenging situations and to reflect on those responses.

In Dolf Zillmann's (1988) article "Mood Management through Communication Choices," he suggests that people often actively select media based on its ability to either enhance or maintain their current emotional states or moods. Zillmann proposes that people are drawn to media that might amplify or alleviate their current mood, seeking content that amplifies positive emotions or alleviates negative ones. For instance, someone feeling upbeat might be inclined to watch a comedy film or play *Super Mario Bros.*, whereas an individual experiencing stress could opt for soothing music, a relaxing TV show, or a calming video game, such as the cozy farming simulator *Stardew Valley* (ConcernedApe 2016). The theory suggests that media consumption can be a strategic and reflective process where individuals make choices to optimize their emotional well-being. However, we may choose a eudaimonic experience for a different reason. We may choose to watch a difficult film, read a biography of a complex individual, or play a game that requires emotional work to complete because it offers something beyond amplification or alleviation. An experience that requires emotional work and reflection on our part may offer us the experience of catharsis. Even when we play a game that requires us to experience unpleasant emotions, and even to fail along the way, the outcome of that journey may be enhanced by its ups and downs, its sense of accomplishment, and catharsis. As in the hero's journey discussed earlier, the trials and the abyss are a part of the process of earning our reward.

In his book *The Art of Failure* (2016), game studies scholar Jesper Juul describes how we choose to play games that cause us to struggle, to fail, and to feel complicated emotions. Juul writes, "We generally try to avoid the unpleasant emotions that we get from hearing about a sad event or from failing at a task. Yet we actively seek out these emotions in stories, art, and games" (4). In essence, what Juul calls the *paradox of failure* suggests that difficult situations, even failing in games, are not a deterrent but a motivator, as games provide a safe and controlled environment where players can experience failure without real-world consequences.

Overcoming difficult challenges and learning from failures in games can actually contribute to a sense of accomplishment and mastery in our lives. Learning scientist Manu Kapur (2008) refers to the playful act of trial and error as *productive failure,* a concept applied in mathematics education, sometimes also called *productive struggle*, perhaps because of the negativity associated with the word *failure*. The idea is to fail forward, as learners employ their own logic and prior background knowledge in generating solutions to problems through experimentation. Playful experimentation in a video game may be on screen as well as in the player's head. Gee (2003) refers to this as the *discovery principle*, which describes how players work through a series of well-ordered problems when in video games. Whereas reflective readings of games and media are not mentioned in these theories, by extension, we propose that working through difficult emotional experiences and readings of games can provide the same kind of productive struggle for players. The experiences of reflecting on our failure to save Joel in *That Dragon, Cancer* or our quest to regain our character's voice in *Gris* are all productive struggles.

Celeste (Maddy Makes Games 2018) is a narrative platformer that engages players in this kind of productive struggle. The narrative follows the journey of Madeline, who must climb Celeste Mountain. Throughout the ascent, players navigate intricate levels filled with hazards and puzzles. The game's deep challenge can also be read as a metaphor for the protagonist's (and game designer's) lived struggles. Although *Celeste* beautifully blends its gameplay mechanics with a heartfelt story of mental health and perseverance, it very is difficult to play. When Farber played, he switched to "Assist Mode" in settings, dialing back the challenge so he could better explore the story. In doing so, he wondered if the easier mode might adversely affect the required struggle to understand the game, or if it would afford slower and more reflective play. With this in mind, Farber journaled his experience of failing in the Mirror Temple, an early chapter in the pixelated peaks of *Celeste*. He wrote:

> I am standing on a platform in a 2D world not unlike *Super Mario Bros*. Soft piano music plays. Theo, my bearded, backpacked guide in front of me, welcomes me with dialogue, "Feeling adventurous?" Madeline replies, "Uh, I don't know. It looks pretty dark in there.

> More like a nightmare than adventure." I am not given a choice of dialogue, just the option to proceed. Yet I wonder, will this be a nightmare? I follow Theo into the darkness, into the cave. First is a hallway, where I jump up over ledges to find where Theo has gone. Then there is a big open room with moving obstacles. I need to ascend higher. I wall-climb and jump midair. I make it through on to a ledge and find Theo's phone. I hope he is okay. The next room is filled with spiky red blobs on the walls and floor. I double jump to get a strawberry on the other side, hit a spike, and die. Instantly, I regenerate and try again. I'm on Assist Mode, but I have to try more than twenty times, and finally, finally, I get the strawberry, catch the moving ledge, and wall-climb some more. Glad I got the strawberry. I just had to have it. I climb up to the next room and see more spikes. Did Theo make it?

Each screen offered Farber a cascade of precarious platforms and daunting obstacles (see figure 5.7). In these initial chapters, he grappled with the mechanics, often mistiming jumps and colliding with spikes in a symphony of failure. Rather than feeling mired in frustration, the game encourages persistence. Later in the game, after repeated failure, Farber was met with a supportive postcard that

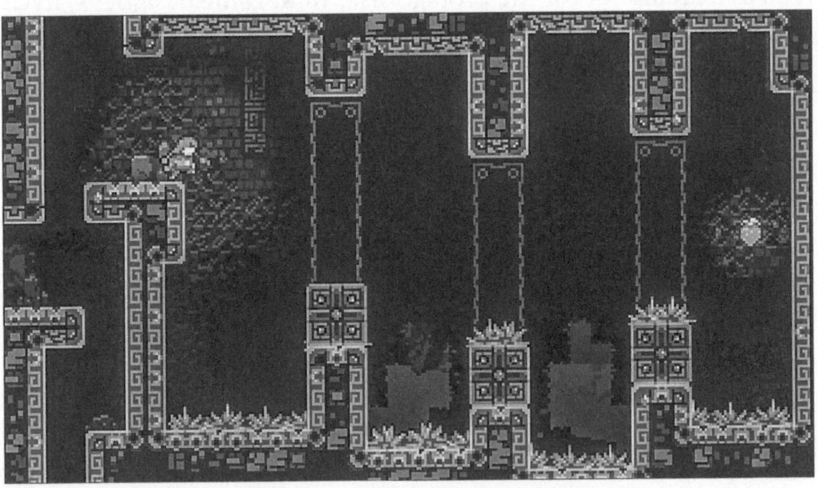

Figure 5.7
Strawberry in the Mirror Temple from the game *Celeste*.

read, "Be proud of your Death Count. The more you die, the more you're learning. Keep going!" Notes of encouragement and relief when reunited with characters on the journey invigorated Farber to continue climbing.

Catharsis refers to the purification or purgation of emotions, often through art or any intense, transformative experience—like Farber's experience in Madeline's improbable mountain climb or Fullerton's navigation of the difficult puzzle platforming of *Gris*. The term has been particularly associated with Aristotle's concept of tragedy in literature and drama. Aristotle believed that witnessing these intense emotions—such as fear, pity, and sadness—in a controlled, fictional setting would allow the audience to process and purge similar emotions from their own lives. Juul (2016) suggests that we experience catharsis differently in games than in theater or written text *because* of the paradox of failure. In other words, because we expect to fail when we play games, we do not quite feel the same cathartic relief as with other media. Juul writes, "We appear to *want* this unpleasantness to be there, even if we also seem to dislike it" (4). But we also expect to experience failure in stories of catharsis and still feel the purge of these emotions. Is cathartic play in games really that different from other forms of emotional drama? As we have seen with eudaimonic media, wanting to experience something that includes complicated emotions can be an acknowledgment that we are ready to grow and learn from that experience. We may want to struggle with a game because we want to learn from it and because reflecting, growing, and learning from an experience can be a cathartic, if not "pleasant" experience.

Celeste's community of players has interpreted the meaning of the game as an allegory for the struggles of a trans person's experience. The designer has confirmed that this is, in fact, canonically the case (Thorson 2020). Although we may feel a sense of exhausted relief in finally landing on a platform in *Celeste*, we can simultaneously feel gratified for the narrative checkpoints in Madeline's journey. We begin to understand Madeline better through her quest to climb Celeste Mountain, which mirrors the challenges faced by individuals navigating their gender identity. In a game like *Celeste*, player failure is part of the experience that can lead us to empathize with the character's journey.

Like the initial stumble and fall that Fullerton experienced at the start of *Gris*, the repetitive failures built into the punishing design of *Celeste* set the player up to feel the depth of the character's struggle and, eventually, the sense of catharsis that is achieved upon reaching each goal. Although a trans player might feel this experience more deeply and personally, Farber was able to experience a version of that struggle through the difficulty of the game's mechanics and even reflect on his own choice to play in Assist Mode as an interesting metaphor for cisgendered players. This seemingly simple affordance helped Farber to perspective-take, deepening his understanding of others. Like diverse books and films, expanded friend networks, and travel, playing different types of games can open sliding glass doors to help us understand ourselves and the experiences of others in the world around us.

As we can see, the ability to reflect on our play is not limited to slow or "easy" to navigate games. Challenging games like *Celeste* or *Gris* can be as emotionally difficult and cathartic as games like *Gone Home* or *That Dragon, Cancer*. Catharsis can exist at the narrative level and in the gameplay. It is the player's ability to reflect on their struggles that creates the true difficulty level of a game when it is read aesthetically. This ability to reflect on perspectives that are not our own shows us how well-read play can heighten our relations with and accountability to others who are different from us, making us better able to participate in the complex and diverse communities of today's world.

6
Playing against the Game

In our discussions around player readings of games so far, we have focused on those that are clearly aligned with the narrative intentions of the game's designers. But what of those that are not aligned with the designer's intentions? What can we make of player experiences that subvert, reject, or purposefully play with the authorial intentions of the game? For example, when a player doesn't pursue the life of a petty criminal in *Grand Theft Auto III* (Rockstar Games 2001) but instead decides to drive a taxi around Liberty City, listening to the radio and picking up passengers. They will never accomplish the goals as set out by the game and they will not follow the arc of the general narrative, but they may have a rewarding and engaging experience playing against the expectations of the designers. Or when a player does not feel represented by the player character in terms of gender, race, or motivations, as is the case for many diverse players who take on the roles of white, male, and otherwise empowered player characters whose situations and motivations may differ greatly from their own experiences. In chapter 5, we discuss the concept that games can act as "sliding doors" for players to enter worlds that they are unfamiliar with—but what of worlds and characters that are familiar and yet antagonistic to a player's own identity?

Why would we want to play in the representation of worlds that deny us our individuality? What can we read from our experiences as an unrepresented player or get from the pleasures of playing in, or against, such games?

Fullerton is a player who often takes on what she thinks of as an "orthogonal" play style in games—an approach that is at odds with the clear intentions of a game. Playing *Grand Theft Auto III* to experience the freedom of driving around Liberty City is an example of this kind of simple orthogonal play. In addition to driving a taxi in Liberty City, Fullerton also played a lot of *Halo 2* (Bungie 2004) with friends, enjoying the multiplayer combat and custom game configurations. However, after the rough-and-tumble combat sessions were over and the rest of the team had signed off, she and her friend Bajeeto (gamertag) often stayed in the game to go "hiking in *Halo*." She recalls:

> The map we often played was called Beaver Creek, and it was a canyon surrounded by rock walls, with stone arches crisscrossing the space so that you could run over them and shoot down on the other team (see figure 6.1). Running across the arches made you

Figure 6.1
Beaver Creek in *Halo 2*.

> wonder if you could find a way to climb up higher. When we were "hiking" and talking over the voice chat, we got the idea that we might be able to climb to the top of the cliffs, so we kept running into the collision boxes, trying to get some purchase on the landscape. Slipping and sliding as we tried to get to the top of the cliff, we finally, surprisingly, worked our way up higher than we'd ever been. Finally, we got to a little level area and were shocked to find a spacecraft up there! We were ecstatic! We jumped all over the spaceship, and it started rocking! We realized we could push it, and we did! We shoved it right over the cliff and watched it tumble down the hillside. It was so much fun. We started talking about how it was as much fun to discover that ship and shove it down the hill as it was to play the actual game. Maybe more. And maybe as much fun as finding something like that on a real-world hike.

"Hiking in *Halo*" has become a favorite metaphor for Fullerton—representative of how players can produce deep play experiences within games that might have little or nothing to do with the intentions of the authors of the game but still evoke deep, memorable, and sometimes subversive gameplay. In British scholar Stuart Hall's foundational communications book *Encoding and Decoding in the Television Discourse* (1973), he argues that media texts are encoded by the creator of the text and decoded by the audience. However, different audiences will decode the text in different ways, sometimes in very different ways than intended by the creator. Hall proposes that audiences will adopt one of three possible positions for decoding a text, each of which will result in a different type of reading. First, they may produce a *dominant* or preferred reading which aligns with the creator's intent. This type of reading may be produced if the audience is of the same age, gender, culture, and so on, which creates an opportunity for them to fill in the gaps in the text with the same underlying assumptions as the creator. On the other hand, an audience may also reject the preferred reading, creating their own *oppositional* meaning for the experience. This may happen if the audience comes from a different age, gender, culture, and so on, and the media contains ideas that contradict their own experience or beliefs. Last, an audience may produce a *negotiated* reading of media experience, which is a kind of compromise between the dominant and oppositional readings, and may result when the audience accepts some of the experience's assumptions but not others (Hall 1973). As with the traditional linear texts that Hall (1973) was considering, we can also look at how players create dominant, oppositional, and negotiated readings of their experiences in games. It may be that games are experiences that can even lead and teach players to create oppositional and negotiated readings more so than a linear text because of the explicit invitation to playfully affect the experience. Going beyond that invitation can be a natural next step for players in the creation of house rules, speedruns, mods, and more.

In *The Death of the Author*, and other works, Barthes (1977), whose concepts of the readerly and writerly texts we discussed in chapter 4, argues that each individual reader's interpretation of the work overrides any "definitive" meaning intended by the author. The pleasures of such readings can range from what Barthes calls *plaisir* to *jouissance*, which roughly translate to "pleasure" and "bliss." For Barthes (1977), *plaisir* is "a pleasure . . . linked to cultural enjoyment and identity, to the cultural enjoyment of identity, to a homogenizing movement of the ego" (9). In other words, *plaisir* is a sense of being one with the intentions of a readerly text, an inclusiveness with the homogenized view of the fictional world. *Jouissance*, by contrast, is a kind of bliss that explodes existing codes, that allows the reader to break out of and reform existing structures from invited interaction with a writerly text. For players whose sense of identity or desire in terms of gameplay is not contained within the potentials of a game, *oppositional play*, such as the creation of new rules or interpretations of existing mechanics, can offer a strong sense of identity creation within open-play experiences like those discussed in *Grand Theft Auto*, but also the in-between round gameplay created by hiking in *Halo*. This kind of play, in its breaking of rules or creation of experiences beyond the author's intent, is directly related to the kind of *jouissance* that Barthes describes.

Other examples of oppositional play might include speedruns of slow-paced games like *Gone Home*. As discussed in chapter 3, *Gone Home* is a game that requires players to slow down and explore the details of home in order to discover what has happened to the family. Running through the game without engaging with each discovery and interpreting how it changes your understanding of the narrative produces a banal and efferent reading of the game. Players may be able to tell you what happened by speedrunning through the Greenbriar house, but they will not feel or understand the motivations and themes at work in the experience. Nevertheless, it is still possible to play this way. In a forty-seven second(!) speedrun of *Gone Home*, one online player is able to jump from the opening moments to the final sequence of the game by knowing the exact unlock sequence (Miekkob3 2013). It's a proof of mastery, on one hand, but it also calls to attention the irony of this kind of play, as Sam's voice pleads with us, playing as her sister, to "understand why I had to do what I did." Of course, having skipped the entire contents of the story in this speedrun, a player cannot understand why Sam did anything at all. It is an interesting thing to note that speedrun communities are very often made up of players who find deep enjoyment from defeating the intentions of not only the game as designed but also the game as experienced *and* the game as understood. Their *jouissance* comes from not only writing the text anew but also from defeating all the intentions of the author of the text.

Another one of the ways that players have historically rejected or opposed the dominant readings of games is by creating their own mods with themes that contradict the original intentions of the designers. *Velvet-Strike* (see Schleiner, Leandre, and Condon 2002) was a modification of the game *Counter-Strike* (Valve Corporation 2000) created by Anne-Marie Schleiner, Joan Leandre, and Brody Condon, which added "protest sprays" that built on the game's existing graffiti feature (see figure 6.2). These antiwar, antimilitary protest sprays allowed players to "take back" the virtual space for protest rather than combat, creating an oppositional experience to the intended hypermilitaristic *Counter-Strike* game experience. This example is an extreme one, however, given that players would need to seek out the Velvet-Strike mod in order to experience this oppositional reading—and anyone who would do so was likely more inclined to be aligned with its antiwar sentiments than opposed to them. But it is an example of how a community around protest can be built in games by oppositional play.

Other examples of players opposing the dominant reading of games lie in the creation of skins and new objects for games like *The Sims* (Maxis 2000) or *Animal Crossing*. When Fullerton played the original *Sims* game, she didn't create her own skins, but she downloaded skins made by other players to import into her game. *The*

Figure 6.2
Screenshot from *Counter-Strike* featuring a spray from the *Velvet-Strike* mod.

Sims was set in a neighborhood that looked like a stereotypical California suburb—homes with yards, sidewalks, and no businesses. The underlying character AI for *The Sims* was tuned to portray situations that matched that stereotypical narrative. The wants and needs of the characters centered around bodily needs (like "hunger," "comfort," "hygiene," and "bladder") and social needs (like "energy," "fun," "social," and "room"). By trying to fulfill these needs, characters simulate the activities of suburban life. Hungry? Stand and look in the fridge for something to eat. Bored? Play basketball. Tired? Go to sleep. Uncomfortable? Maybe you have to pee. One of the most interesting and value-laden variables was "room." If a character didn't like the options available to them in the rooms you had decorated for them, they would be unhappy until you bought them more or different objects—is your Sim not happy with a bookshelf? Maybe a television will make them happy? Better make some money and go shopping! The underlying rules of *The Sims* created a value system that not only simulated a suburban neighborhood but also the material hunger and spiritual ennui of late capitalism. Perhaps unknowingly, or perhaps intentionally, the game typically evoked readings of want: I want a bigger house for my Sims, I want a pool, I want a nicer couch or a better television, I want, I want, I want . . .

But players, immediately upon the game's release, began creating the already mentioned custom skins and uploading them to the internet for others to download and apply to their game. Many of the skins aligned with the game's original intention but were simply customized to look like the player's family and friends. Or to look like famous TV and film actors or characters. Once skins were downloaded, they could be applied in any household and combination. And they could be used to tell stories. The scrapbook feature in *The Sims* allowed players to take screenshots of their play sessions and annotate them with captions. Some of the most fascinating scrapbooks to emerge from this feature included readings of *The Sims* that used custom skins to tell stories of family traumas, including abuse or neglect. Far from the perfect suburban household simulation provided by the creators, players used *The Sims* to work through personal issues and tell their own stories in the game. They created oppositional experiences that were completely orthogonal to the imagined happiness of *The Sims*'s intended play. In his 2001 keynote talk at the Game Developers Conference, game designer Will Wright demonstrated several of these scrapbooks and spoke with a kind of stunned wonder at the experiences that players had created far beyond any of his team's original intentions. "That's not in *The Sims*," he stated bluntly, and with bemused wonder at how such things could emerge from the simple wants-and-needs system of this little suburban capitalism simulator (Wright 2001).

When Fullerton played the original *The Sims*, she didn't create a scrapbook about trauma or abuse, but she did play against the game's intentions in a different way. Here is her reading of the game from her game journal:

> I have always been a science fiction fan, so when I saw that some players had created skins for *Star Trek*, *Star Wars*, and *The X-Files*, I downloaded them and set up a whole neighborhood of sci-fi characters. The way a neighborhood works in *The Sims* is that each house is a different save game, but if you are playing one house, the characters from another house will come over and visit your house randomly and socialize with your current Sims. Sometimes, they even move in. But one time, I was playing *The X-Files* house, and a story emerged that was so unbelievable that I started taking screenshots to make sure I never forgot it. *The X-Files* skins included Mulder, Scully, and two alien kids—a boy and a girl. The alien kids were hilarious—both were bald with big alien eyes but otherwise looked like regular kids in jeans, T-shirts, and sneakers. Mulder worked as a Paranormal Investigator—that was an actual career path in the game—so he worked at night and would come home early to watch the kids. Scully had a day job, so they didn't overlap a lot. I had bought them a bunch of stuff related to space and aliens in the store that I thought they'd like, including a rocket launcher for

the kids' room. I didn't realize you shouldn't put a rocket launcher in the house! One day, the kids were playing in their room before Mulder came home, and they set off the rocket launcher. It caught fire and the little alien girl was caught in the flames! Mulder came home and raced upstairs and into the fire, trying to save her. But they both burned up and the Death character came and took them away. Scully and the alien boy were so distraught. I buried Mulder and the girl in the backyard and created a little grave garden for them. Scully and the alien boy would go out and weep by the graves. They were inconsolable. I didn't know what to do. Nothing could comfort them. Nothing I bought from the store made them happy (see figure 6.3).

Finally, I got an idea. I went up to the main menu of the game and created a new household—the Mulder Clone household—and moved a copy of the Mulder skin character into it. Then, I went back to *The X-Files* household and waited for the Mulder Clone to come visit. When he did, I helped Scully to meet him and they became friends right away! She treated him just like Mulder. They went in the hot tub and hung out every day. They were superhappy. But the alien boy would not accept the Mulder Clone. He would weep by the grave and look through the telescope every night, searching the stars for the real Mulder. The Mulder Clone tried to play basketball with him, but he wouldn't have any of it. And then, something crazy happened.

Figure 6.3
Fullerton's *The X-Files* scrapbook in *The Sims*.

> The original Mulder started haunting the house! Every night, when Scully and the Mulder Clone were watching television or were in the hot tub, the sad greenish ghost of the original Mulder would walk through the house. And the only Sim that seemed to notice him was the alien boy. Somehow, using *The X-Files* skins and this crazy suburban living AI, I had evoked the beginning of *Hamlet*!

There is so much possibility for reading a simulation game like *The Sims* in an oppositional or negotiated way that it is a kind of low-hanging fruit for this discussion. But what of games that are working hard to tell us one type of story? How can we learn to play in ways that evoke readings beyond those intentions? In literature classrooms, oppositional readings may actually be taught alongside the dominant reading of a text, provoking learners to explore underlying themes or relationships that don't, at first glance, appear to be the dominant aspects of a text. University of Northern Colorado literacy professor Jim Erekson shared thoughts with us about standard practices in literary criticism, in which teachers often ask students to reread passages and to reinterpret based on new perspectives and multiple interpretations. Erekson spoke about how he uses the well-known children's book *Where the Wild Things Are* (Sendak 1963) with his college literacy education students. The students often come away with a fairly simplistic reading of the book, in which a young boy, Max, is sent to his room without supper for causing a ruckus in his home. Max imagines that his room transforms into a mysterious jungle filled with wild creatures, where he is hailed as the King of the Wild Things. Erekson uses the book to show his literacy education students how, when applying different lenses regarding power relationships, the book can evoke several different readings, allowing them to see that the book is more complex than they had originally thought and is actually exploring difficult issues regarding power and control in relationships between Max, his mother, and his imaginary wild subjects. Max is working through his relationship to power and control in a magical world, where he may wield power himself but can also experience the loneliness and regret of his choices. A similar oppositional theme can be read in the game *Lost Words*, described in chapter 2, where the child protagonist fantasizes about having agency in a magical world after her real world overwhelms her with grief.

Beyond the simulations or mods that we've already examined above, narrative games can also be protected spaces where we can work out our issues through play and through oppositional and negotiated readings. We have already seen in earlier chapters the way in which games like *Lost Words* and *Gris* can lead us on journeys through loss and grief. And how games like *Edith Finch* can allow us to play with powerful ideas around death and fate. But what about games in which the narrative is not intended to lead us on such a journey, and yet players find the space and inclination to evoke oppositional and negotiated readings? As mentioned above, Fullerton is a player who often finds herself playing against the intended narrative of games—this may be for a number of reasons, including gender, background in literary and media studies, and perhaps an overall interest in exploratory play versus pure competition. When she was playing the first *Red Dead Redemption* (Rockstar Games 2010), for example, she often ignored the quest lines dealing with the story of John Marston, a former outlaw trying to go "straight" in the violent world of the Wild West. Instead, she spent much of her playing time exploring the desert and riding through the night on her horse. After playing, she journaled:

> One of the early quests had you breaking a wild stallion, and once you do, you can make this horse your own. I felt like I had a special relationship with the horse and kept it for a long time. I would go out riding at night in the desert, even though I knew there were dangerous people and animals out there who would try to kill me and the horse. I got to be very good at avoiding or killing these threats. But one night, I wasn't lucky or maybe I wasn't paying enough attention. We were attacked by coyotes that I just didn't see. The horse tried to protect me, and even though I eventually

> did kill the coyotes, the horse was fatally wounded and died. I was devastated, as I felt like I had a special relationship with it after all the time we'd spent together. I wanted to bury it, at the very least, but the game did not offer a way for me to do that. So I simply hung around it, mourning for a while. I tried walking far away to see if it would disappear, at least. I didn't want to think about more coyotes coming to eat its corpse. But it did not disappear, at least not right away. Finally, I gave up and walked to the next town. When I got there, I saw that the horse had respawned in town, but it broke the spell. I didn't believe that this was "my" stallion. I chose another horse to ride instead and went back to playing the main quest line, as my experience with the stallion made me too sad to go back out into the desert again. Ultimately, I remained unmoved by Marston's journey and stopped playing the game before he redeemed himself, unable to find as much interest in this man's experience as I had in my own private journey or in the hints by NPC character discussions about the experiences of Indigenous people or the collision in the world between new technologies and the wilderness.

Similar to Fullerton's oppositional play in the original *Red Dead Redemption*, nature writer Nicholas Lund (2019) took his own oppositional approach to playing the sequel, *Red Dead Redemption 2* (Rockstar Games 2018). Lund spent his time looking for birds rather than riding stallions, but he has an equally personal and oppositional experience. In an article for the National Audubon Society, he writes, "The first time I see ravens, I flush them out of an alpine meadow carpeted with wildflowers. I pause to watch the flock fly off towards the distant, snow-capped peaks, trailed by their echoing croaks . . ." (Lund 2019, para.1). So begins Lund's obsessive goal to track down all the birds in the game (see figure 6.4). "I spent most of my time finding birds," he writes, "and was impressed with the breadth and relative accuracy of the species represented. Birds change with habitat: Roseate Spoonbills and Great Egrets feed in the bayous of Saint Denis. Laughing Gulls and Red-footed Boobies roost along the coast, while eagles and condors soar over mountain

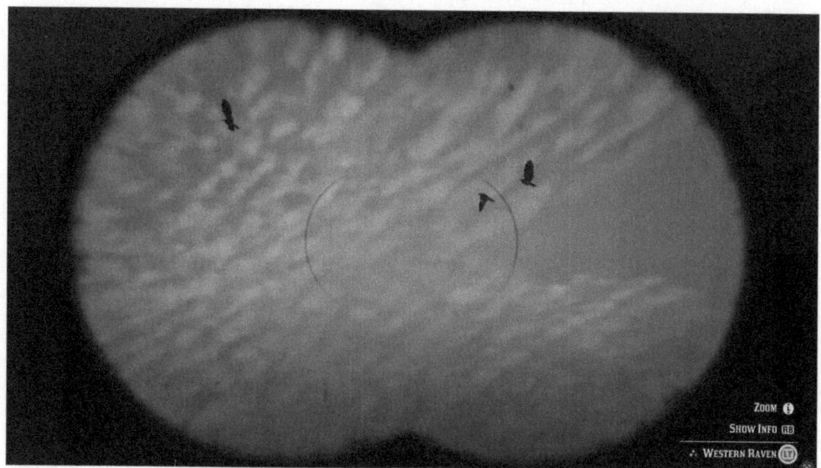

Figure 6.4
Bird-watching in *Red Dead Redemption 2.*

peaks. Each of these are crafted with accurate field marks and habits. There are dozens of species I couldn't even find, including Carolina Parakeets, Ferruginous Hawks, and Pileated Woodpeckers. Like real life birding, you're never guaranteed to see anything" (Lund 2019, para.1). There is a story in *Red Dead Redemption 2,* of course, but if you are reading Lund's account, you might believe that it is the story of an ornithologist living in the late nineteenth century, seeking out and documenting the birds of the Old West.

A provocative perspective on oppositional play comes from queer studies of video games. Game scholar Bo Ruberg (2017) questions accepted notions that players are only playing to win a game. They write that we can understand "queer play" as going beyond the ability to play at gay marriage or choose transgendered avatars. Ruberg suggests that players can "queer" straight games by playing them against the intentions of their creators. "Queering the seemingly un-queer is a particularly touchy, and therefore particularly powerful, practice when it comes to video games, an artistic form with close ties to its historically homophobic player base" (Ruberg

2017, 199). Ruberg touches on something in their discussion that is critical to our concept of reading games: that avid game players are often criticized for caring too deeply about their play. "What does it mean to read a game too closely?" asks Ruberg. "'Too close' implies intimacy, inappropriate contact, poking and prodding and pressing—an almost sexual and certainly ludic encounter with the video game itself. It means caring too deeply. Gamers, of all people, know what it's like to be told by those who do not share their passion for games that they care too much. These intimacies are queer intimacies, alternate visions of the control–freedom dynamic—the intimacy between player and game, between flesh and the controller in our hands" (2017, 201).

As Ruberg points out, there are a number of games that now allow players to choose queer storylines, such as the romanceable character options within mainstream AAA games like *Mass Effect* (BioWare 2007), *Dragon Age* (BioWare 2009), *Cyberpunk 2077* (CD Projekt RED 2020), *Assassin's Creed: Odyssey* (Ubisoft 2018), and *Assassin's Creed: Valhalla* (Ubisoft 2020). These offer players a variety of gendered choices for creating romantic relationships across various combinations of characters. Players cannot only read those combinations in relation to their own experiences and assumptions, but they can also make choices that align the game outcomes with those experiences, play against them, or negotiate between them. If you are playing a male character pursuing the witty Dorian Pavus in *Dragon Age: Inquisition* (BioWare 2014), for example, you can help that character, who is estranged from his father because of his sexual orientation, to reconcile with his father, or not, depending on your desired outcome and reading of the game. One might think of these examples as negotiated readings because they accept some of the intentions of the game authors while also allowing the player to read and evoke their own experiences.

But Ruberg's suggestion of queering games has more in common with oppositional readings than negotiated ones. They discuss the pleasure that gamers take in "epic failures" like fiery and explosive car crashes in a race car driving game and wonder about what this implies about "different" or "queer" ways to play. Of course, the designers, in creating the spectacular explosions and crashes of *Burnout Revenge* (Criterion Games 2005), the game that Ruberg (2017) analyzes, understood that players would love this kind of failure and so invested a lot of energy in these glorious explosions. Because of this understanding and intention on the part of the designer, we might argue that the very inclusion of these epic fail states in the game design makes them not different, oppositional, or queer. Because a designer knows their game will be queered and designs for it, does that render the opposition co-opted? It is a bit of twisty, self-referential logic, and Ruberg asks the question in this way: "Is it possible to fail at a game that you win by failing, to fail against the system in a game that encourages you to fail toward it?" (2017, 206). Their answer is yes because in the case of the crashing scenario, you can crash less violently, less spectacularly, and overall with less aplomb. But what of a game that encourages you to fail but also encourages you to succeed? A game that, like some pieces of sophisticated literature, is unreliable in its intent and therefore provokes the player to mistrust and misread their own situation. How can we know if our reading is dominant, oppositional, negotiated—or even queer—if we don't understand, or can't trust, the intent of the designer?

The Stanley Parable (Galactic Café 2011) is a game that demonstrates this problem using a classic literary technique: the unreliable narrator. As with some literary texts, games can also lead us along what seems to be an intended path, guiding us with tutorials, cues, and sometimes narration. And, like our relationships with the unreliable narrators of literature, our relationship with the experience of reading such a game can become muddled, filled with uncertainty about the facts of the story, the possible outcomes and themes, and just what we are supposed to make of the experience as a whole. When we learn about this technique in middle or high school literature classes, we may be taught it in the context of a naive narrator, like Huck Finn (Twain 1884), who questions why he is doing the "wrong thing" to help the runaway slave Jim, even as we understand that he is actually doing the right thing. Or we may learn about it when we read a story like the *Tell-Tale Heart* (Poe 1843), told from the perspective of a madman who reports on terrible things that he may or may not have done. We may be taught to pay attention when narrators like Nick in *The Great Gatsby* are coloring their reports of the action with their own perspectives and values. But rarely would we encounter a situation where we, as readers, are embattled with a narrator who is actively lying to us, provoking us, and at the same time trying to placate our fears that he is doing anything of the kind.

This is the situation in *The Stanley Parable*, a first-person branching narrative that puts the question of whether or not the player should trust its narrator—that is, do as he describes or not—at the center of its core experience. In fact, questioning our relationship with the narrator is the main activity of the game. In *The Stanley Parable*, we are introduced to Stanley, a character who works in an office pushing buttons on a computer all day in response to instructions—a thinly veiled metaphor for playing games. Stanley comes to work one day and realizes that he hasn't received any instructions for some time. When he leaves his office to investigate, he finds the office empty; no other workers are there, though there are signs of them having been there and having left in the midst of a normal day. Papers are scattered on desks, and a lighted projector in the conference room shows a slide on how not to get fired. Soda cans and other detritus common to a working office are strewn around, but there are no other people. As we explore, our choices are accompanied by a very proper, if slightly pompous, narrator's voice describing what "Stanley did" in the past tense. If we do as Stanley "did," the story progresses along. If we choose to do something different from what Stanley apparently "did" in some other play of the game, the narrator will critique our choices: "This was not the correct way to the meeting room and Stanley knew it well" or "Stanley was so bad at following directions, it's incredible he wasn't fired years ago." When Fullerton played the game, she immediately took offense to this officious narrator telling her what to do:

> At the first real choice point, I come to two doors (see figure 6.5), and the narrator tells me that Stanley took the one on the left. I don't want to follow directions. I turn around and try the door I just entered from, but it's locked. So I choose the only other option of resistance—the door on the right. I go through it and am chastised that this isn't the correct way to the meeting room. It's the way to the employee lounge. I go there and it's empty, so I start just walking around, trying to find another way to go—any way except the way the narrator is telling me to go. He's getting mad at me now. "Look, Stanley," he says, "I think we've gotten off on the wrong foot here." I keep ignoring him. Finally, he says something that intrigues me: "Stop trying to make every decision by yourself," he says. "I'm not asking for me; I'm asking for *her*." I have no idea who he is talking about, but the way he says it lights up some kind of trigger in my gamer brain. Is this a character I should be interested in? Someone I should care about? Someone I can save?

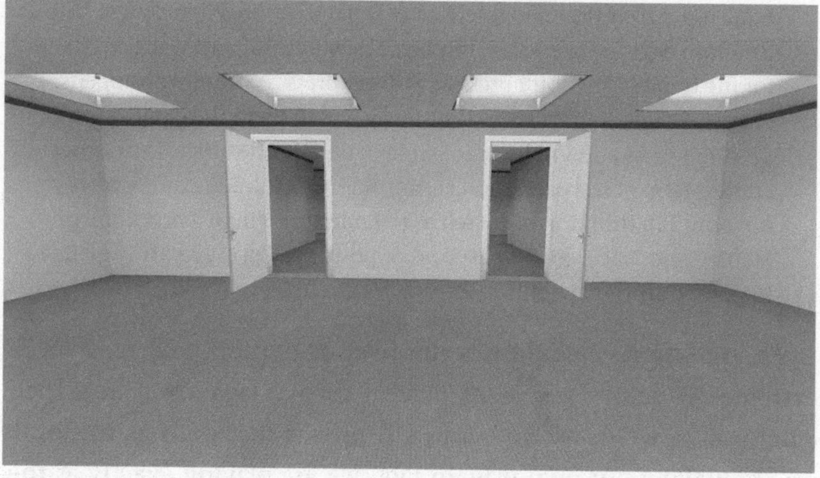

Figure 6.5
Choosing between two doors in *The Stanley Parable*.

Even though I've been playing against the game, I start listening. And then, as I continue searching, I find myself shut in a dark room with a bright light shining on a yellow phone. The phone is ringing. I know I'm supposed to pick it up. But I've been trying to resist the game. I can't pick it up if I'm supposed to. But I'm so curious because this might be "her." I know it will be "her." Because there is no one else it could be. I can't help myself. I pick up the phone. I hear her voice—sweet, a bit too sweet—telling me she's putting something in the oven. She's my wife? My girlfriend? I don't know, but now I'm in the game again, not fighting it. And the game cuts to my apartment, where she answers the door . . . but it's all a trick. She's a blank mannequin, an undressed game model, not even animated. She answers the door, and the narrator crows—he's gotten me to believe that Stanley had a life of some kind beyond the office, beyond pushing buttons. I wasn't playing against the game after all. I'm trapped in its layers of confusion.

The narrator has me questioning whether I should push the buttons that I'm told to or not. He's telling me the entire story of the game is simply in Stanley's mind—that he was so bored he imagined a day when no one was at work when he got up from his desk and stopped pushing buttons. But it's all a lie. In reality, he is just pressing the same buttons he always has. To prove it, he instructs me not to press the button the next time the interface tells me to do so. I don't press. The interface begs me to press *P*, but I resist. Everything just waits. Waits for me to press *P*. I don't press . . . I don't press . . . nothing happens. Finally, I can't help it. There is nothing else to do in the game. I must press *P*. I press and I'm back at Stanley's desk in the office, in another endless loop of resistance and conformity. I'm thinking of my own life now. I'm thinking of myself as the narrator. I'm in a metaloop of Stanley and Tracy, conformity and opposition. Can I ever truly be free in play? Can I escape this mad paradox of choice and control?

The Stanley Parable pushes the idea of oppositional play to its extreme—it challenges us as players to play against it and then laughs at us when we do because it proves that even as we think we are playing our own way, in fact, we are playing exactly as the narrator expects us to, that we don't have an original idea at all. But even as it laughs at our attempts to act originally within the game's constraints, it can't actually take away our ability to think and feel differently about the game and to evoke our own personal reading of the battle of wits between the narrator and our game. We may not be able to *act* in opposition to the narrator's expectations (or the designer's intent), but we can still be trying to *think* in opposition, to *read* and *play* in opposition to that intent. Our intentions in play are, to a certain extent, as important as the actual situation. We may be playing against a system that is already structured to respond to oppositional play, such as *The Stanley Parable*, or we may be playing against a system that does not respond, accept, or otherwise change or break when we play against it, like the example from *Red Dead Redemption*. However, our experiences of playing in opposition to a system are still valid. In fact, the sense that we are acting in a way that was *not* anticipated by the designers may give even more validation and power to such experiences. When we look at YouTube videos of players capturing "broken" moments of gameplay, we hear and see a kind of joy and exultation in the commentary that suggests Barthes concept of *jouissance*. In these cases, it is as if the "game" they are playing is not the game itself but rather the metaexperience of finding and capturing errors in the game software. One fun example of this can be seen in a YouTube video of a *Red Dead Redemption* glitch which replaces bird animations with characters, making it look like there were people flying around the desert landscape (Brad 2010).

Oppositional play offers players an inverted power relationship to the game itself, one that attempts, through claiming our own personal readings as primary and above the authorial intentions of the designers, to break out of the implied power that all rule-based systems of play impose over their participants. In the oft-described paradox of play, we submit ourselves to a system of rules and constraints in order to experience the kind of "freedom" that these voluntary constraints can offer. Within the loose restraints of a game system, we can experience a form of freedom because we are not entirely bound. Were we not bound at all, our freedom would not be discernible; however, when we are slightly bound, what freedom we have is highlighted, as is any opportunity we have to think or act in opposition to the implied parameters of the game. And so, within the constraints of a game, within that paradoxical situation, acting out, performing, or reading our play against the intents or expectations of the designers takes on a sharply understood sense of absolute freedom. Stewart Brand, editor of the *Whole Earth Catalog* and one of the founders of the New Games movement, wrote in his essay "Theory of Game Change," "You can't change a game by winning it, going by the formula, or losing it or refereeing it or speculating it. You change a game by leaving it, going somewhere else and starting a new game. If it works, it will, in time, alter or replace the old game" (1976, 137). This provocative idea might seem to naturally send us down the path of creating new games, games that provoke new kinds of play experiences. This is a good path, and one that many game designers, including the authors, have been down. But here, we are suggesting something different. Rather than making new games, which we also believe is a good idea, we are proposing playing and reading existing games in new ways.

This tactic is one that is more aligned with DeKoven's concept of the well-played game. DeKoven suggests that another way to change a game is to become a "better" player. By better, however, he does not mean a more expert player or a player who wins a game more than others. DeKoven (2013) writes that games are "social fictions, performances, like works of art, which exist only as long as they are continuously created. They are like plays or songs or dances, belonging to some special sphere of human activity, which clearly lies outside the normal reality of day-to-day living. They are not intended to replace reality but to suspend consequences. They are not life. They are, if anything, bigger than life" (21). With this in mind, he comes to the determination that to play games well is to be "at our best. We are fully engaged, totally present, and yet, at the same time, we are only playing" (DeKoven 2013, 22).

Sometimes, DeKoven suggests, a game as it has been designed isn't what we need—right then, in that moment, or ever again. Maybe we've exhausted the potential of a game, or maybe we've changed our way of thinking about what we want and need to adjust the rules. Changing a game, opposing your current reading by addressing how you approach it or what rules you choose to follow from it, is completely acceptable in DeKoven's view of a well-played game. In fact, more than acceptable, it may be imperative to oppose a game if the experience it is creating isn't provoking you to be at your best. For DeKoven (2013), "the definition of playing well is the result of an ongoing process of negotiation and renegotiation. It changes as we do, sometimes drastically, sometimes subtly" (64). Throughout this book, we discuss situational and playcentric models of understanding games and players in relationship to one another. The player evokes the game by playing—whether that evocation is aligned with the dominant reading, is in negotiation with the dominant reading, or is in opposition to it. But we are suggesting now that sometimes a game needs to be entirely co-opted, changed, and adapted by the players to provoke an experience where they can play it "well," or as DeKoven (2013) would say, in a "state of excellence and health" (22). DeKoven gently rejects the idea that playing a game as designed, to use Upton's (2017) phrase, is the goal at all. He embraces the "bending" of rules, the "well-timed cheat," and the idea that there is no "*the* game" at all if we are to be completely open to it. Whatever we are playing at, however, we are playing at it, is *the* game.

Game designer Navid Khonsari shared an anecdote with Farber's students in 2019. A few years earlier, Khonsari was the cinematic director at Rockstar Games, where he worked on *Grand Theft Auto*. As it happened, there was a player who experienced a game differently than intended by its designers. Khonsari recalled a response from the player who created her own game out of the existing game. He said,

> When I was in Iran in 2006, I met this young woman who'd been playing *Grand Theft Auto: San Andreas* (Rockstar Games 2004). She said that America must be the most amazing place to live, which is interesting because most of the stuff that is said about *Grand Theft Auto* is that it is very, very violent. And this was during the time when US forces were present in Iraq and Afghanistan. When I asked her what she meant by that, she said that when she is in the game, she doesn't try to be a gangster. Instead, she hops in her car, listens to any music that she wants to, buys any clothes that she wants, and goes to any fast-food place—she even goes and works out. She can do all these kinds of things, freedoms she was not able to have within her own country or in her own real life. For me, that moment was monumental in recognizing the power that video games have to change people's thoughts and opinions of one another and close the gap between us.

Cortez et al. (2022) published a study of existing games used by player communities to rewrite their own narratives. More specifically, they found groups of players who self-organized Black Lives Matter protests within open-world games during the summer of 2020. Examples included a protest outside a police headquarters in *Grand Theft Auto V* (Rockstar Games 2013) and marches in *The Sims 4* (Maxis 2014) and *Animal Crossing: New Horizons* (Nintendo 2020). In these instances, the games were subverted to become spaces for speculative activism and Blacktivism (Cortez et al., 2022). Grassroots activist movements in games gave the researchers "hope and possibility" when they saw "Black people leverage their histories as a resource in the present to imagine radically new Black Futures in games" (Cortez et al. 2022, para 1).

And so, with DeKoven as our guide, we can come to the conclusion that pushing back on the rules of a game, on the intended reading of a game, bending or breaking that reading to our satisfaction and needs, is part of playing a game well, and so it is part of reading a game well too. When we push back on power—when we use *Animal Crossing* as a place to hold graduation ceremonies during a global pandemic or a social justice protest, or we speedrun slow games like *Gone Home*, or just go hiking in *Halo* or bird-watching in *Red Dead Redemption*—we create oppositional readings that can be even more meaningful to us as players than the dominant readings that lead us through more conventional moments of catharsis. And, as we push back on the power of games to control our readings of situations and experiences, we become more mindful and thoughtful citizens of play and of the larger world.

7
The Pleasures of Reading Games

It seems appropriate at this point to bring in the voices of our own community of play to share how they respond to and read games. We have said that our ultimate hope for player-response theory is to help develop more sensitive and articulate player communities so that they might become not only better players but also better people and better citizens of plural and democratic societies. Over many years, each of us has encouraged our students to reflect and journal their experiences with games. Fullerton's *Game Design Workshop* (2024) includes an exercise in game journaling in its first chapter that asks readers to "dig deeply into the choices you made, what you thought and felt about those choices," and to analyze "one moment of gameplay that stands out" (11). Additionally, we have cultivated a list of peers—professional and scholarly—whom we have talked with or heard speak about their own deep responses to play. While writing this book, we asked a number of these players from our combined communities to take a moment to submit a small sample of "game journaling" to us for this discussion. The prompt we gave these players was quite open-ended:

> We are reaching out to you because we think you are the kind of person who thinks and feels a lot while you play video games.

> Similar to journaling, we're looking for first-person submissions of moments of emotionally interesting game experiences. Something that resonated with you, long after playing the game. We've included a couple of examples from our own play to spark your imagination. We're hoping you can take a moment to think about a moment of gameplay like these, and submit it to us in this form. Don't worry about it being "articulate" or "well written"—just focus on the emotions, what happened, describe it to us like you're describing a dream you had to a friend or writing in a personal journal.

This collection of player-response journaling is not meant to be comprehensive, and does not represent a scholarly study of the form by any means. However, by looking through these responses, we can see, even from our small sampling, that these accounts demonstrate many of the same core pleasures we see in literary experiences. They also represent a wide variety of game genres and situations of play—everything from abstract puzzle games to hardcore combat, and from single-player and coplayer to multiplayer experiences.

We have organized these player responses by using the work of Perry Nodelman, whose writing informed our discussion in chapter 2 about how some children's literature is structured to teach us how to become closer readers. In the influential textbook *The Pleasures of Children's Literature* (2003), Nodelman, with Mavis Reimer, includes a list of the "literary pleasures" that we get from reading children's books, situating them as a form of literature alongside books written for adults. This list is written to illuminate the aesthetic joys of children's literature; however, in many ways, it pertains equally well to games as a form of literature. Nodelman himself writes, "Books for children often include pictures as well as words, and these visual texts have their pleasures also; and the same might be said of films, TV shows, video games, and any other imaginative art that includes visual elements" (n.d., para 1). The list begins with some of the deep sensory pleasures of experiencing sounds of words and images, which we relate to the basic verbs of gameplay as discussed in chapter 2. Beyond these sensory pleasures, the list then digs into a wider variety of responses that include having one's emotions evoked, making use of existing knowledge and strategies of comprehension, recognizing gaps and bringing our knowledge to fill them, finding a mirror for oneself, and experiencing the lives of different people (Nodelman and Reimer 2003). Many of these pleasures are ones we have discussed at length in earlier chapters. There are also pleasures around the appreciation of literary structures and the insights they bring, including the pleasures of perspective-taking and stepping into imagined worlds, the pleasures of gaining insight into history or different cultures, the pleasures around narrative formulas, and the pleasures around the breaking of those formulas (Nodelman and Reimer 2003). Below, we walk through each of these pleasures ascribed to the realm of the "literary" below, demonstrating that they can be found in the aesthetic readings of many players as well.

For clarification, we did not ask contributors to directly address any of the pleasures described on the following list, but after receiving them we found that the submissions sorted themselves quite easily. A version of each of Nodelman and Reimer's (2003) pleasures is quoted below in bold from Nodelman's website (https://perrynodelman.com/the-pleasures-of-literature/), and the player responses are block quoted. Where we have permission, we have shared player responses with attribution and, where requested, with anonymity. We have also included some additional moments of gameplay from our own readings.

What we hope to show with this wider range of examples from our own community of play is the way in which aesthetic readings of games can demonstrate some of the same transformational aspects as familiar literary experiences do. Also, how exploring these oft-ignored aspects of play will lead us to becoming better readers of games and, by extension, to enrich our understanding of the world, of ideas, and of the experiences of other peoples. Once we are engaged in such a community of shared experiences and ideas, we are able to practice more advanced skills of social dialogue around these experiences and build our own communities of play.

The pleasure of experiencing sounds and images in and for themselves—as pure sensory activity outside and beyond the realm of shared meanings and patterns.

This core pleasure of sensory activity is one that is often cited when discussing games. *Game feel*, as described by Steve Swink (2009), and the *juiciness* of game feedback, as described by Jesper Juul and Jason Scott Begy (2016), lie within the canon of ideas about what makes games pleasurable. But here, we see a slightly different take on the concept of sensory pleasure. In this journaling submission, Grace Collins, founder of Snowbright Studio, writes about the soothing pleasure of *Puzzle & Dragons* (GungHo Online 2012), a simple match-three tile-moving game that would not, at first, seem to be the kind of game that might provoke an aesthetic reading. Collins shows here, though, that what a player brings to the game experience can create a sense of sensory bliss and evoke the very essence of an aesthetic experience. Collins recalls:

> When we had our first child, I was a nervous wreck. So much responsibility! Part of that responsibility was waking up at night to change, feed, and rock to sleep . . . Those long nights of rocking in the nursery! I had to stay awake, rocking without keeping the baby up. I turned to my phone and a little mobile game called *Puzzle & Dragons*. For months, almost every night, I'd be silently sliding colored orbs around the screen in one hand while waiting for my child to fall into a deeper sleep in my arms. The colorful parade of anime deities kept my thoughts from wandering . . . ruminating, really . . . on the anxieties that face new parents. Iron deficiency? Match 3 and unlock Anubis. Daycare drama? Match 6 and unlock Apollo. Is Paul Ryan shutting down the government again? Match a few more and unlock a golden egg. When our kid finally started sleeping through the night regularly, my time in *Puzzle & Dragons*-land waned.
> Now, looking back, it's hard not to miss those times. Whatever the

> complexities of the day, there was nothing for my child and me to worry about at night. Just a warm blanket and a rocking chair.

Is this an example of how games can provide an escape through flow? Yes, certainly, but the layering of concerns here in this lived experience—parenthood and politics all wrapped up in the aesthetic reading of a mobile puzzle game—transcend a simple escape. It demonstrates our theme that the evoked experience of a game goes beyond authorial intent and can become personal and poetic even in the most abstract scenario of play.

The pleasure of words themselves—the patterns their sound can make, the interesting ways in which they combine with one another, their ability to express revealing, frightening, or beautiful pictures or ideas.

We can look beyond Nodelman's reference to "words" and think, in this case, about the verbs of play as discussed in chapter 2. In one of the earliest Well Played sessions at IndieCade 2011, Fullerton discusses her experience playing the abstract musical puzzle game *Halcyon* (Zach Gage and Kurt Bieg 2010) and discovering the pleasure of its meditative and yet difficult gameplay. She writes,

> Each level of *Halcyon* has several strings, which make musical tones when you touch them on the iPad screen. They feel like the strings of a harp. On each string float "currents" of different colors. When two currents of the same color are approaching each other on a string, they are drawn together immediately until they collide and disappear in a wonderfully simple and satisfying way. When two currents of different colors approach each other on a string, they create a dissonant warning wave and sound, which gets stronger and stronger as they get closer. You can move currents by drawing paths from one string to another. When a current meets a path you've drawn, it will be diverted to the new string and the path will disappear. So, you are constantly caretaking this little musical world, striving for beautiful tones and trying to make sure dissonance disappears. There's no score on the screen while you play, and there

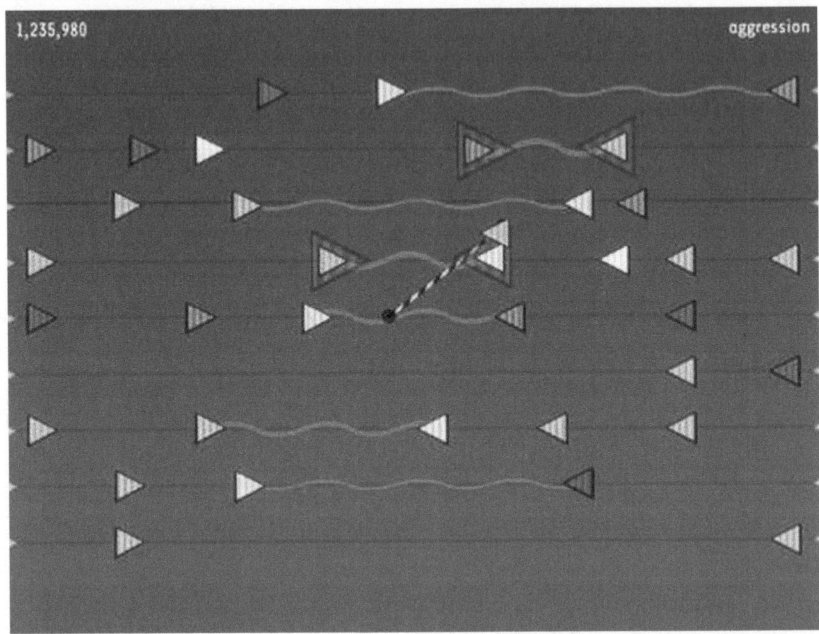

Figure 7.1
The pleasure of abstract patterns in *Halcyon*.

is no enemy other than dissonance. Each current has a partner and once met, they disintegrate. It's like some kind of fatalistic musical mating dance. At the end of each level, the play space is empty, pristine. Early on in the game, each level only has a few strings and a couple of colors. The pieces move at a leisurely pace, plodding along like some kind of intricate quadrille of dancers. Later, it is made difficult by the number of strings involved, the variety of colors of currents, and how quickly the currents are moving. Both the sound and the visuals become messy, dissonant, complex. We go from a formal quadrille to a complicated modern dance performance (see figure 7.1). But as we finally move all currents to meet their partners, the field once again becomes clean. After the greatest danger has passed in a level, we're left with a cleanup period that is like the quiet sweeping up of a theater after an ecstatic abstract performance.

The pleasure of having one's emotions evoked—laughing at a comic situation, being made to feel the pain or joy a character experiences.

USC Games graduate student Maynard Hearns writes about his game experience from *Season: A Letter to the Future* (Scavengers Studio 2023), in which players are Estelle, a woman traveling the world as it comes to an end and documenting the experiences in her journal. The section of the game that he writes about is only a few minutes into the experience, but nostalgia and pity for a fictional world that he has never known and a mother who is not his own provokes an extremity of emotion. The tug of emotions here is intentional—it is the hook of the game. Players must care about the world that is ending and the mother who will be gone with it if they are to take the rest of the game to heart. Here, it is the activity of choosing which parts of that world his fictional mother will forget that Hearns writes about as he finds a deeply felt pleasure in taking on the responsibilities of the game world. Hearns writes,

> "What is it about our young eyes that imbue everything with meaning?" These words were spoken by my character's mother. We are making a charm for the journey, and I've been selecting items from home based on the senses: touch, smell, hearing, and with the one in my hand, sight. As a cost of making this charm, my mother must forget a part of my childhood, something she has cherished. I witness her brow pinch, grasping at what is slipping away. A distinct betrayal happening before my eyes. Out the front door and into the world, the fright of forgetting has nestled deep in me. I pounce on the sound of wind chimes and water. Foley and Camera in hand, I feel my chest tightening as I move toward the sounds of music in the square, too conscious of my footsteps. "Don't race. Quiet. You'll miss it." Everything around me takes on an urgency, as does every word ever to be spoken. How quickly did I come to miss this world, less than twenty minutes after hitting "Start"? I linger. I weep. I turn my mother's words over again in my mind: "Imbue everything with meaning."

The pleasure of making use of a repertoire of knowledge and strategies of comprehension—of experiencing mastery of what the text expects of its readers.

This pleasure of mastery is, of course, a core pleasure for many game players. We quote an anonymous USC Games graduate student on their experience in *Xenoblade Chronicles X* (Monolith Soft 2015), as they are both surprised by a moment of exploratory play in this action role-playing game but also energized by it, sounding confident and remembering the moment with a kind of efficacy that exudes the pleasure of mastery. The student shares:

> Early on in my adventures on Mira, I remember sprinting through the forests in the first part of Noctilum and spotting a massive, half-drowned, and long-abandoned machine in the middle of a lake surrounded by a circle of rocks below me. Adventurer that I was, I decided to take the plunge and swim to this interesting locale to add it to my map. As I watched my characters swim toward the machine, I began to wonder about the history of this broken machine. "How was it destroyed?" I wondered. "Which alien race made this thing? What did it look like when it was active?" My final question was answered once I reached my "landmark," who, sensing my characters' arrival, began to move, and Uncontrollable blared on my headphones to inform me of my mistake. I had awoken Go-rha, the Guardian Deity, who proceeded to one-shot my party before I could react with more than a laugh.

The player says alongside their journal entry:

> It's worth noting that in the Xenoblade games, interesting locales like where Go-rha decided to go to sleep are generally called vistas or scenic spots—areas where the player can obtain an EXP reward and a map completion bonus for visiting these areas. I wasn't expecting anything from this broken-looking robot lying abandoned in the middle of a lake other than something to mark on my map, and I certainly was not expecting a fight!

Again, the player's tone exudes both shock and surprise at the encounter but also the kind of assurance in their own ability that makes such experiences pleasurable.

The pleasure of recognizing what reader-response theorists call gaps—aspects of literary texts that require readers to bring knowledge from outside the texts themselves in order to make sense of

them—and often, learning the information or the strategy needed to fill them, thereby developing further mastery.

We discussed the concept of gaps in chapter 2 when we described the ways that players must often fill in meanings—both narratively and systemically—as they produce their readings of games. These kinds of gaps provide moments for the player to miss something at first, then have an epiphany about their play, about the formal aspects of the game, and to construct moments of response that become part of their own stories. Here, USC Games Professor Richard Lemarchand describes such a moment, where his gap of understanding became a beautiful moment of loss in the game *Subnautica* (Unknown Worlds Entertainment 2018), an underwater adventure game where you have crash-landed on an alien ocean world filled with danger and beauty (see figure 7.2). Lemarchand writes,

> I built a base in the glittering shallows next to where my escape pod had come down. It was small but homey, with convenient storage cabinets and an aquarium full of my favorite fish. I was recklessly extending the base when suddenly it ruptured. Water began to rush

Figure 7.2
Building a base in *Subnautica*.

> in, filling it in seconds. I had no idea how to deal with this: how to stop the flood or repair the base. (I'd decided to play the game without searching the internet for tips.) Panicked, I flailed around, trying and failing to stop this disaster. In defeat, I floated to the surface and looked down on my inundated former home. But I hung on to hope and started over. I spent an evening building a new base next to the broken one, and in doing so, noticed a number on the screen indicating the stress on the base. That helped me figure out how to reinforce a base and build even more deeply as I explored the beautiful, fascinating world of *Subnautica*. I love this systemically rich game, with its intense atmosphere of loneliness, hope, and wonder.

The pleasure of the pictures and ideas that the words of texts evoke—the ways in which they allow one to visualize people and places one has never actually seen or think about ideas one hasn't considered before.

One of the fascinating effects of the COVID-19 pandemic was the way in which so many players turned to games to feel like they were together with others. Weddings, graduations, and other virtual gatherings made communities feel like they could experience each other's presence even while far apart. For college students, entering programs like the one at USC Games, this also extended to visualizing and "being" in a place they had never been before, meeting and getting to know other students from around the world whom they had never met before. As this undergraduate, who wished to contribute anonymously, writes in their game journal,

> During the pandemic, my first year at USC was online, so I had to meet new people and make friends through the internet. After months of interacting with each other through voice and video chats, my friends and I decided it would be fun to play on an online *Minecraft* server where we, as virtual USC students, explored our college campus in *Minecraft*. When we first started playing *Minecraft* together, the game gave us a sense of physicality and connection, such as playfully "punching" each other in the game even though we were miles apart and even across the globe. Our interaction with

> the *Minecraft* world and each other gave us a "tangible," shared experience of USC that was missing during the pandemic.

The pleasure of finding a mirror for oneself—of identifying with fictional characters.

As discussed in chapter 5, the pleasures of finding mirrors for oneself in gameplay run as deeply in games as they do in literature. We may see ourselves in our own player character, or we may see others in our lives in relationship to our character. Here, USC student Diego Melendez reads a moment at the end of the first-person shooter game *Titanfall 2* (Respawn Entertainment 2016), where a character, BT, sacrifices himself for the player. BT, Melendez said in submitting this journal entry, reminds him of his father. Melendez shares:

> Were we not invincible? Did we not break time itself? Did we not slaughter our way through hundreds, no, thousands of our enemies? Your voice is as scratchy as your imaginary beard as you tell me we have done well and reassure me. We were finished. End of the game; Over, done, 100-percented. Is that not how it was supposed to be done? I'd abandoned hundreds of your kind in countless ways: nuked them, left them to die, forced them to be my shield in battle. But I couldn't leave you. We fought factions together; you taught me how to play. A father to his son. You nearly died, you nearly fell, but you stayed with me. It was supposed to be a second wind, not a final hurrah. "Protocol 3: Protect the Pilot." I let this titan fall; I can't let him.

The pleasure of escape—of stepping outside oneself at least imaginatively and experiencing the lives and thoughts of different people.

We find the pleasure of escape referenced often in discussions of games as well as all forms of storytelling. Stepping away from our own lives and cares for a moment is often thought of as running away from our worldly problems. Here, however, in a journal entry about the adventure game *Outer Wilds* (Mobius Digital 2019), USC graduate student Anooj Vadodkar calls to mind a different kind of escape: the beauty of a moment of play where all is lost for this game universe, for this cycle of play, and yet the poignancy of witnessing a world come to its end is itself a pleasure. In *Outer Wilds*, the player is an explorer in a solar system whose sun will go supernova in twenty-two minutes. Every time loop gives the player a new chance to play witness to the lives and people of this doomed system. Vadodkar recalls:

> During one of the early loops of my playthrough, I found myself on Brittle Hollow, captivated by the sight of a planet forming around a black hole. So captivated that I missed a jump and plummeted toward what I thought was my inevitable doom because what else could a black hole be? I waited and waited, bracing for the start of the new loop until . . . I fell through. To my utter shock, the black hole hadn't killed me; it tossed me to the other end of the galaxy through a white hole. I quickly looked for my ship to see if I could get this information to anyone, only to realize for the first time just how big this oh-so-tiny galaxy was. The deep red of the sun told me that there was no way I could reach my ship in time, and the white hole prevented me from taking the short route. So I did the only logical thing I could think of and pulled out my signalscope to listen to the music of the galaxy while I waited for my next chance. I still whistle the tune that I heard beyond those stars.

The pleasure of resisting.

In some sense, all games require a kind of resistance—because we are constrained by the rules of the game, we must resist in order to participate at all. So, this pleasure, which in a purely narrative experience might simply be to hope against what is happening, or to resist allegiance or empathy with a main character or situation, is more strongly highlighted in our experience of a game. We resist in order to play. But in some games, that resistance can be even more direct. In this reading of *1979 Revolution: Black Friday* (iNK Stories 2016) by Fullerton, resistance is both required and a matter of fate. In this interactive narrative game about the Iranian Revolution of the 1970s, you play as Reza, a young photojournalist who has returned home from Europe to find Iran on the brink of revolution.

He is torn by opposing allegiances—his family, his friends, and his hopes for the future of his country. In the scene described here, the player must make a critical choice (see figure 7.3). Fullerton writes,

> As I explore the streets, I suddenly become part of a student rally. Hundreds of people fill the streets I have just been wandering peacefully. There is an energy and excitement. My friend Babak is clearly aligned with the protesters and wants me to see what he sees. Bibi, the student leader, is an impressive and articulate young woman up on the stage calling for a free Iran. She introduces an older man, Abbas, who takes up the call for freedom. As he speaks, I am encouraged to join the crowd and cheer for him. But I am not ready to be part of the movement, so I don't cheer. Babak keeps pushing me to support Abbas, but I keep silent, preferring to stay neutral. I do take some pictures of the event because it is so exciting. Even when my cousin Ali shows up and tells us he's joined the revolution and is ready to fight for it, I resist his urging and try to keep my neutrality—after all, I am a photojournalist. I feel like my job is to observe, not to take sides. But when soldiers show up and start to disrupt the gathering, things get more complicated. What should I do? What should I think? What does neutrality mean in a situation like this, where the right to protest peacefully is being destroyed? Babak and Ali each

Figure 7.3
Reza must make a choice in *1979 Revolution*.

> push me to go their way: Babak wants peaceful resistance, and Ali wants me to join in throwing rocks at the soldiers. I can't resist both of them. In the end, I choose not to throw the rock because I believe in peaceful resistance. But the soldiers don't care, and the protest erupts into violence anyway.

The pleasure of story—the organized patterns of emotional involvement and detachment, the delays of suspense, the climaxes and resolutions, the intricate patterns of chance and coincidence that make up a plot.

We have discussed a number of narrative pleasures in earlier chapters, and it is a well-recognized problem in games that we both desire these kinds of pleasures and yet find them sometimes difficult to perceive in the same way that we do in linear media. Often, our experiences with stories in games are a pleasurable mash-up of what Katie Salen and Eric Zimmerman (2004) call *embedded narrative* and *emergent narrative*. We see that kind of mash-up of suspense and anticipation in this journal entry from USC graduate student Youbin Wang in his description of a plot twist in the puzzle-platform game *Portal 2* (Valve Corporation 2011). In this scene from the single-player campaign of *Portal 2*, the player is Chell, a silent protagonist, who is tested by the accidentally reactivated AI, GLaDOS, from the first game. Here, Wang describes the inciting incident of the story—the crossing of the threshold in terms of the hero's journey—where Chell and GLaDOS fall together into the lowest levels of the abandoned laboratories of Aperture Science, from which Chell must work to escape, as GLaDOS works to rebuild the lab. Wang shares:

> The elevator crashed, and I fell down a bottomless, circular pit. I looked up and the falling elevator was not far above me. What is at the end of this pit? Will I be killed by the fall? Why was there such a bottomless pit underneath Aperture Labs? It made me very nervous. At this point, GLaDOS, strapped to a potato, appeared in front of me and humorously informed me that I was wearing Advanced

> Knee Replacement components and that a fall would not harm me. This eased my nerves slightly but made me even more curious—where exactly was the end of this pit? The descent is fast; the sights all around me fly by. The occasional signs around me hinted at the distance I had fallen. The walls around me changed from neat lab iron to stone walls in disrepair. What had caused this change? What was the Aperture Science facility doing so deep underground? That's when I saw a couple of wooden planks across the center of the pit. Before I had time to react, I crashed into it, the boards cracked and I lost my senses.

The pleasure of storytelling—the consciousness of how a writer's point of view or emphasis of particular events shapes one's response.

We don't usually think of the point of view of the game designer or writer when we think of stories in games—but rather the player's influence on how a story is told. These pleasures can work together, however, as we see in this moment from *The Legend of Zelda: Tears of the Kingdom* (Nintendo 2023) submitted by USC graduate student Linhan Li. Here, Li regrets her actions as a player because of how they affect Princess Zelda. This moment of possibility was created and planted by the designers specifically to tempt players for just this reason; however, it is the consciousness of the player that highlights how this moment of storytelling can contain both a pleasure and a regret. Li recalls:

> After the Princess swallowed the secret stone and transformed into a dragon, she voluntarily chose to be imprisoned within time. Her tear, representing the last trace of "human will," fell on the land of Hyrule. Where her tear landed, a cluster of Silent Princesses (a type of flower) bloomed. As an adventurer, I've become skilled in gathering, so I instinctively plucked one. In my backpack, it displayed a brief description of this flower: "Endangered Flower Revered by Princess Zelda." There were no specific hints about its use, unlike other materials. Suddenly, I deeply regretted plucking this flower. The flower, symbolizing Princess Zelda's will, was snapped by me, a practical-minded puppet. I've always been one to explore the

> boundaries of games. Yet, at this moment, I really wanted to preserve the integrity of this story.

The pleasure of structure—the consciousness of how words, pictures, or events form cohesive and meaningful patterns.

Finding patterns in the structure of play is, again, a deeply discussed pleasure. We refer to this in our discussion of *Tetris* and flow in chapter 5. The act of seeking out structure can be related to puzzle mechanics in games but also to narrative, to the exploration of terrain, to understanding combinations in strategic play, and in the kind of player deconstruction that we see in this journal from Professor Andrew Phelps, director of American University's Game Center. Here, Phelps recalls playing the early computer role-playing game *Bard's Tale: Tales of the Unknown* (Interplay Productions 1985) with his friends and father.

> I first "played" *Bard's Tale* on a Commodore 64, looking over the shoulder of the older, cooler kid who lived down the street in California. Then we moved to New Jersey, and I was the "new kid" with no friends. But I got a computer that year and started playing *Bard's Tale* myself, and I remember my dad started playing it with me. I would move the characters and take care of battles, but he was the cartographer and mapped our moves on graph paper and kept track of the mazes. We'd work out systems of "OK go [direction]," and then I'd read the description of the new square and whether there were walls in any given direction. We laughed when we first figured out the spinner traps and the silent teleports. Probably fifteen years later, I found those old pieces of graph paper during another move, and I was floored by how much they meant to me, by how much Skara Brae (a city in the game) meant to me. It was partly because it was playing with my dad, partly because it was those first months without a lot of friends, and partly because it was such a cool, early game that was *D&D*-like. I can still close my eyes and picture that world and giggle when I see references to 4×99 berserkers.

The pleasure of one's awareness of the ways in which all the elements of a literary work seem to fit together to form a whole.

When we come to the end of a well-read game, we may experience a kind of holistic moment where all the elements and themes of the experience seem to come together for a moment to illuminate one another. This kind of pleasure is easy to recognize because it is a kind of peak moment of play—where our struggles and challenges meet our understanding in a kind of epiphany of sorts. We see that kind of awareness here, in a journal from USC games student Farai Halle discussing his experience in the action role-playing game *Nier: Automata* (PlatinumGames 2017). In *Nier: Automata*, you play as multiple characters across multiple playthroughs, following the viewpoints of characters on both sides of a war between alien-created Machines and human-created Androids. This experience is from what is often described by players as the "true" ending of the game, in which the player is asked to sacrifice their save game for the good of future players. The themes of the game are about love and struggle, or "agaku" as described in Japanese by its director, Yoko Taro, which might seem strange in a game about warring machines. However, in the game, the machine and android characters revere long-dead human thinkers and philosophers, taking names like Pascal (after Blaise Pascal), Simone (after Simone de Beauvoir) and Jean-Paul (after Jean-Paul Sartre). The ability for players to sacrifice their game for unknown other players across the world was inspired by a Coca-Cola campaign, where drink machines in India were connected via livestream to machines in Pakistan, encouraging the two peoples to overcome their political rivalry. The campaign made a strong impression on Yoko, who adapted the idea into in-game messages of encouragement from players across the world (Minotti 2018). Halle shares:

> Playing through the final ending of *Nier* left me stunned. The final boss was ruthless, I was dying over and over again, and it was getting very late. I'm thinking to myself, "How am I going to beat this?" After failing many times, words of encouragement started to appear on the screen from other players giving me hope that it somehow

Figure 7.4
Choosing to sacrifice your save game in *Nier: Automata.*

> was possible. But I still could not beat it. The game gave me one final prompt, asking me if I wanted to accept help. I did, and soon after, with the help from other players, I was seeing much success. The music started to roar, and it nearly brought me to tears. After beating the boss, the game presented me with one final decision (see figure 7.4). It was one of the most memorable moments in a game for me ever. If I wanted to help someone else in the world like others came to help me, I had to make a sacrifice. No game had asked me to do this ever, and I stared at the screen for so long, but I felt solace in my decision. I still think about this game every day.

Alternately, the pleasure of becoming aware of ways in which the elements of a literary work do not seem to fit together to form a whole.

We can also find pleasure in the tragedy of a well-read game that does not work out as expected. Just as we find pleasure in consistency, we can also find a kind of pleasure in the realization that we've been led along a path, only to find a harsh reality at its conclusion. Here, game designer and author Ian Schreiber describes such an experience at the end of the role-playing game *Final Fantasy VI* (Square 1994). Schreiber recalls:

> The moment when we're on a floating island chasing down Kefka (the main antagonist of the story) for what feels like the final confrontation. Having played many computer role-playing games, until this point, I think I know what's coming because it's always the same. We're the heroes. We go around beating up random mobs, leveling up, and getting to the point where we can take down the final boss, who is inexplicably just sitting around passively waiting for us; then we beat him up and save the world. That's how this works. And all the signs are there: the Emperor is dead, there are no other obvious antagonists other than Kefka, we've just fought our way through a special dungeon detached from the rest of the world, the background music is different from anything else encountered. So far, we're already twenty hours in . . . this should be it. Except it isn't. We won the battle and escaped off the island alive, but we didn't stop Kefka. As we escape, the entire world is pretty much destroyed. And I realized at that moment that nothing would ever be the same. In the game, nothing would be the same because the Apocalypse actually happened, the bad guy won, and the best I could possibly do at this point is to eventually topple him and then start the slow process of rebuilding society. But outside the game, things would also never be the same: whenever I play a game in the future, I have to acknowledge the possibility that I might do everything right and still have terrible things happen.

Schreiber acknowledges the pain of realizing that a video game could tell a story in which the player completed the game but did not "win" the story. This shock was new at the time and created the possibility that players might find a kind of cathartic pleasure in dramatic failure, much like the pleasures of other tragic endings. Our investment makes the failure keen and real to us, and the cautionary message it evokes is more realistic than we might expect.

The pleasure of understanding—of seeing how literature not only tries to mirror life but comments on it and encourages readers to consider the meaning of their own existence, either by agreeing or disagreeing with the meanings the text seems to be supporting.

Like Schreiber's moment of realization above—that a story can seem to be leading us to one place and yet take us to another—there is also a pleasure in seeing how an experience can comment on our lives outside the game. Game producer and composer David Warhol connects his play of *A Mind Forever Voyaging* (Infocom 1985) with the headlines he sees every day and continually reevokes his experience with that early interactive fiction game. *A Mind Forever Voyaging* is set in 2031, and you play as a sentient computer instructed to run a simulation of a citizen in this alternative United States after initiation of a "Plan for Renewed National Purpose." As Warhol describes, the plan doesn't go as expected, and each iteration, a decade further into the future, produces more and more unexpected results. Warhol shares:

> I played the role of an AI in a simulated world ten, twenty, thirty, forty, and ultimately fifty years in the future. Each decade's "simulation" was created using societal anecdotes taken from the prior decade: dining experiences, art gallery viewings, department store experiences . . . and, most impactfully, newspaper headlines. As I progressed through the decades, a headline thread that started with "Immigrants flooding over US Borders" became more and more dystopian with each decade: "US Authorizes Permanent Immigration Internment Camps," "Shoot to Kill at Border Deemed Constitutional," and ultimately "US Executes Peremptory Strike in Mexico Successfully Killing 10,000 Potential Illegal Immigrants." To this day, I still look at newspaper headlines with an eye toward, "What trend does this suggest, and if it continues, what will it be in ten years? Twenty years? Fifty years?"

The pleasure of gaining insight into history and culture through literature, either by accepting or rejecting the text's presentations of history and culture.

There are many examples we could give of gaining insight into history through reading games—especially when it comes to the history of warfare. But the example we have here is a more subtle one: that of encountering and gaining insight into another culture through an experience with a game. Erekson, mentioned in chapter 6, describes his reading of the narrative platformer *Never Alone*, also known as

Kisima Iŋŋitchuŋa (Upper One Games 2014). This game is based on a traditional Iñupiaq tale, "Kunuuksaayuka," and tells the story of a young Iñupiaq girl named Nuna and her arctic fox as they search for the source of a blizzard that has ravaged Nuna's village. As the player searches, they are rewarded along the way with cultural insights from elders, storytellers, and community members. As Erekson points out, the connection to these real-world elements gives real stakes to the game scenarios. Erekson states,

> When figuring out difficult obstacles, I had to go through multiple deaths to learn my way. Unlike any other game, I felt distressed EVERY time I died. This was mostly because of the specific audio and animation for the character's death. But also because the dangers felt more real to me than in other games (see figure 7.5). This distress was interesting and engaging, though I worried whether it might stop other people from persisting. I felt like the dangers of the Arctic environment were present, and the cultural knowledge and skills in the interlude videos gave me a sense of real stakes in surviving. The mythological creatures that came after me (or even the ones that helped me) were genuinely frightening in ways that haunted me for days afterward. I usually find big bosses annoyingly

Figure 7.5
Chased by a polar bear in *Never Alone*.

> tropey and clichéd. The ones in this game made me feel like I did in childhood nightmares.

The pleasure of recognizing forms and genres—of seeing similarities between works of literature.

In earlier chapters, we've talked about several games that reference their literary inspirations directly, including *What Remains of Edith Finch*, *Lost Words*, and *Walden, a game*. In each of these, there is a pleasure for players to recognize those similarities and the calls back and forth between the desire to play and the desire to read. Here, game director Chris Floyd, in a personal email to Fullerton, describes how he responded to the connections between the book *Walden* and the game *Walden*. Floyd writes,

> It felt like I was being challenged to "mine" all of Thoreau's words out of the world, in the arrowheads but also the text for all the bushes, trees, landmarks, and so on . . . it made me want to revisit Thoreau's writings.

The pleasure of formula—of repeating the comfortably familiar experience of the kinds of stories one has enjoyed before.

In games, as in literature, there is a comfortable pleasure in reexperiencing stories we have heard or played before. Even as game scholars often discuss the importance of uncertainty in gameplay, we should also recognize that games, like fairy tales or genre literature, sometimes can be equally as pleasurable when we know what happens and what to expect. Here, Phelps, who shared earlier in this chapter, describes his emotional reaction to replaying *World of Warcraft Classic* during the COVID-19 pandemic. Phelps recalls:

> I was working in New Zealand and had only been there about a month. We went into lockdown, and lockdown there was very different from anywhere else—you weren't allowed to be outside unless you could prove you were going to or from the grocery or pharmacy—and in my case, breaking those rules would mean arrest and deportation. It was awful. And *World of Warcraft Classic* had hit

> the scene, and my old guild started playing, and I honestly cried to see Azeroth again. It was an instant teleportation to a better world, another life. Seeing that old guild tabard was just . . . everything in that moment. I'd go on to make lots of New Zealand friends as well, but those first couple of weeks of lockdowns, before the government started allowing "bubbles" (social groups for those who lived alone)—returning to Azeroth was everything.

There is also a pleasure opposite to formula.

Whereas *otome games* (story-based romance games) might at first seem to be the essence of "formula," when we think about them in relation to the larger landscape of video games, they are, in many ways, completely different from what we expect of a "formulaic" video game. There are no enemies but rather objects of desire to woo; no combat but rather conversation; no direct conflict but just finding the best way to a character's heart. Even players themselves can be surprised by the depth of experience they may have with the simple experience of an otome game. Here, graduate student Bernice Wang is surprised by the true feelings they experience for a fictional character in *Code Realize: Bouquet of Flowers* (Aksys Games 2018). Wang writes,

> So, I know that otome games sometimes get a bad rep, and they're essentially one really simple gameplay loop: read, make a choice, read, maybe collect a picture, and so on. However, I was speed-reading through this game during the peak of lockdown, and I must have finished it in less than two days, playing constantly and completing each character's route. I became incredibly immersed in the steampunk world, and in the middle of the night, sitting there in pitch dark except for the screen, I wooed the character St. Germain, an elegant, mysterious gentleman far from my usual favorite type. I can never forget how I felt during the final scenes of his story. I barely remember the actual events, let alone the other characters' plot lines, but my heart hurt so badly for St. Germain. I sat there crying, shocked because I had no idea how such a low-stakes game would impact me so much. I felt like this person had to be real because how could I feel this much for a fictional character?

As suggested a number of times above: the pleasure of seeing through literature, of realizing how poems or stories attempt to manipulate one's emotions and influence one's understanding and moral judgments in ways one may or may not be prepared to accept.

As Wang notes in the reading above, we can be moved by game experiences that we don't expect, and we may not be prepared for the kind of feelings that some games provoke in us. Perhaps we suddenly find ourselves, as Wang describes, affected by a fictional character in a way that surprises us. Or, as graduate computer science student Noah Schwartz describes here, perhaps we must accept our failure in a role that games typically allow us to play. Schwartz describes his experience in the looping storyline of *The Legend of Zelda: Majora's Mask* (Nintendo 2000). In this action-adventure game, the player continually replays a three-day cycle of events, learning to control the flow of time by playing songs on our Ocarina, a wind instrument. Failure to solve all the characters' problems in each cycle is core to the experience of the game, and the emotions that come with failing are part of the bittersweet pleasures of this game. Schwartz writes,

> Each day, the music gets faster. Each day, characters have new dynamic dialogues. They look up. First, they deny, then panic, then accept. The most horrifying part is the acceptance. Everything I've done in the course of those three days comes to a sudden halt as dread and panic sink in. The enormous monstrosity of the moon hangs above, covering the entire sky. Every side-quest, every character I rescued or aided or made smile, all gone to waste. I was hopeless to save them. And though I may save myself by warping back in time, I'm just running. Running and leaving them doomed to the moon's fate. I failed. I failed as a hero, and I failed as a player. I deny this thought. I panic. Then I accept it. I accept my own cowardice and defeat. I accept that everyone I cared for, everyone I spent these past fifty-four minutes helping, is doomed. I leave. I save myself. And I play the hero again—the hero I know I'm not.

The pleasure of exploring the ways in which texts sometimes undermine or even deny their own apparent meanings. Reading for this

kind of pleasure is the basis of the kind of literary theory called deconstruction—an awareness of the constructed nature of texts that allows readers to perceive the incompleteness and artificiality of the construction and what the texts, therefore, consciously or unconsciously take for granted without offering support for.

As we show in chapter 6 when we discuss oppositional play, players can undermine the meanings of a game, but games like *The Stanley Parable* can purposefully undermine their own meanings and provoke a natural deconstruction of the player-game relationship. Are we to follow instructions or not? In this moment from a "fail state" in the game, Fullerton experiences the kind of awareness of the text that provokes pleasure in its own artificiality. She shares:

> I make my way into the mind control facility. It is filled with TV screens, each with a number on it and images of each employee's desk. The narrator is telling me what Stanley felt—his realization that his whole life had been under someone else's control. But even as the narrator exclaims that Stanley couldn't believe that, I do believe it. I can feel my own life being controlled by the game, by the computer I am sitting at, by the internet I am connected to, and all the systems of school and work and government that know my name and have my number. I am Stanley, and I am doomed. Maybe I can find a way to make it work for me. I walk up to the system power controls. The narrator is telling me that this is my moment to turn off the system and free everyone and myself. But I don't. In a moment of contrariness, I turn the system power back on. I bring the mind control system back online. "Oh, Stanley," the narrator berates me, "you didn't just activate the controls, did you? You were supposed to let it go, turn the controls off and leave. If you want to throw my story off track, you'll have to do better than that. I'm afraid you don't have nearly the power you think you do." I'm playing this game, but I'm also thinking about the game of my life and my relationships with all the technologies and systems in my life. Turning them off won't work. Turning them on won't work. How can I live within this paradox of control? I feel the ideas in this game expanding my mind as I think about how it is doing what it is doing and making me think and do both what it wants me to do and what it doesn't want me to do. It's beautiful.

The pleasure of developing a deeper understanding of one's responses and of relating them to one's responses to other texts and to one's understanding of literature in general.

Nicholas Fortugno, director of Gaming Pathways, at City College of New York, who we mentioned in chapter 5, has a background in English literature and a longtime interest in the relationship between story and games. His description of a moment in *Ico* (Team Ico 2001) is informed by that understanding. *Ico* is a critically lauded action-adventure game where you play as a young boy sacrificed by his village because he was born with horns and left imprisoned in a giant fortress. Here, Ico meets Yorda, a girl also imprisoned in the fortress, and the two must escape the fortress together, fighting off the shadowy figures that attempt to draw Yorda back. Praised for its integration of story and interactivity, this reading from Fortugno captures the way that our response to a game can change our approach to understanding games in general. As Fortugno describes,

> In *Ico*, the game state is saved when your companion Yorda, whom you've been guiding through a dangerous castle, sits on a sofa at your direction. Yorda is a constantly present companion in the game, manifested as a vibration through the controller as you run, representing her getting out of sync with you as you travel together. The pulse of the controller becomes a haptic reassurance of her presence. Late in the game, Yorda is taken by the shadow creatures that haunt the castle, and you must spend the last act of the game rescuing her. However, the moment she disappeared off the bridge, I realized I couldn't save the game anymore. Without Yorda, there was no save functionality. That meant I had to complete the game in that sitting. At the same time, as I moved forward to find her, I painfully felt the absence of the controller's pulse. That moment was profoundly moving for me as it was an expected expression of synergy between narrative, gameplay, and feedback. The game had reached a desperate moment where I lost my companion and needed to save her, and this was reflected both mechanically (I couldn't save, so I couldn't walk away) and physically (the haptic presence of the character was removed when it had been occurring several times a minute during the rest of play). This scene changed the way I think

about how games tell stories and taught me new ways of embodying narrative in interactive elements.

The pleasure of sharing experiences of literature with others. In games that are created to be played together, there is, of course, the pleasure of competition and rivalry, but alongside that, there is the pleasure of bonding and camaraderie. Every multiplayer game, at its core, is cooperative—because to play, we must all accept the rules together. So, even in competition, there is what DeKoven (2013) calls *coliberation*. Sharing our gameplay experiences may mean describing them, but it can also mean living them and creating them together. Many of the games we have discussed in this book have been single-player experiences, with notable exceptions like *Halo* and *Journey*. However, multiplayer experiences can be read just as deeply as any others. Here, Andrew Goldstein, an adjunct professor at USC Games, talks about a moment in an early *World of Warcraft* session where his guild faced a great challenge together, without resources or information, and prevailed. He compares the sense of camaraderie that he felt to the sense of being on a championship sports team. Goldstein writes,

> The sheer size of the Molten Giants was enormous compared with my tiny character. Two of them stood at the entrance to a vast raid dungeon called The Molten Core, where Ragnaros the Firelord reigned. It was daunting, to be honest, as forty of us traversed a gigantic online dungeon filled with an abundance of nasty baddies. But there was this sense of adventure, of not knowing what was going to happen, which was one of the purest, most exhilarating, intoxicating, and exciting sensations I had ever experienced. But what made it sacred was that it was a secret. The player base of the game was small, and few had even ventured this far into the game. YouTube didn't exist yet, so information and knowledge were a valuable currency. As a group, we had to figure out different strategies and tactics to get through each encounter, and many times we failed. But when we succeeded in beating a monster that weeks ago, we believed was insurmountable, the emotions and joy were

> so absolute. Even twenty years later, I remember those moments of success as if I was part of a championship sports team, one who defeated Ragnaros the Firelord.

The pleasure of discussing with others their responses to texts one has read.

As we have worked on this book, we, as authors, have engaged in the pleasure of discussing our responses to games repeatedly. We have found that our different backgrounds and tastes in media, games, literature, sports, and more, make our responses to games interesting to compare. One example was our responses to the game *1979 Revolution*, discussed above. Both of us have used the game in our classes and have played and read the sequence described above. We have also both invited game director Navid Khonsari, quoted in chapter 6, to discuss the game with our classes. Fullerton's experience of playing *1979 Revolution* was colored by her memories of watching coverage of the events in Iran during that time on television. Her "baggage" as an American high school freshman in 1979 made her fascinated to see another side of the Iranian Revolution. She recalled coming home every day after school to watch the coverage of protests and the discussions of the hostage crisis beginning in November 1979. Playing the game as the character of Reza many years later in 2016 gave her an entirely new understanding of those protests, which are one of her earliest memories of being engaged with world politics. Both Fullerton's and Farber's classes were equally engaged by the game, even though the students were many years younger and had no personal memories of the historical events themselves. They were moved by Khonsari's accounts of doing background interviews with those who had participated to create the characters for the game, and shared their own hopes for playing and creating games that might move players to become activists and engaged participants in current issues. Playing and responding to the game as part of a community created a positive feedback loop for all involved—developers, players, authors, and subjects—that would not have occurred if each had remained in isolation.

Many gamers love to share their response to games, but the depth and tone of this sharing can be constrained by the communities in which gaming is typically discussed. To feel safe enough to share our emotional responses to games, we need models and communities where these kinds of experiences are valued, respected, and part of our expectations of what gameplay offers us as individuals.

The pleasure of joining the community formed of writers and taking part in its ongoing conversation. All literature and all experience of literature is tied together—a network of ideas and stories, images and emotions. Literary theorists call this intertextuality. Every time you read a text or discuss your response to a text with someone else, you become part of the network. You learn more about the components of the network and, in your own response and conversation, add something to it. All readers and all people who discuss their reading are in the process of making literature, of making it mean more to themselves and to others.

This is the culminating idea of what it means to read a game well: as with literature, all our experiences with games are tied together in a network of responses, stories, and emotions. What Nodelman refers to here as "intertextuality" might also be thought of as the larger community of play. To paraphrase his statement above: every time you play a game or discuss your lived experiences of play, you become part of the larger community of well-read players. All players who discuss their reading of games are in the process of creating the literature of games, of making it mean more to themselves and to others. In the next chapter, we discuss strategies for becoming a well-read player of games and becoming part of this larger community of games.

8
Becoming a Well-Read Player

As we see in the preceding chapters, there is a deep and important beauty to playing games aesthetically and to valuing the type of experiences that aesthetic readings of games produce. To echo Upton's (2017) call for a manifesto for playing games in ways other than trying to win them, we are calling here for a revaluation of what deep gameplay is, how we speak about it and learn from it, why it is important to us as humans, and how it can transform us in ways, as Upton points out, that simply winning games cannot. We insist that games themselves cannot be fully appreciated as an aesthetic form until we learn to value *all* the experiences they offer, not just their systemic and competitive experiences. We are making a strong comparison to literature here because of its relationship to the foundational concept of literacy, which is now understood as a multimodal set of skills that crosses media and aesthetic formats. Games, like literature and other forms of expression, can evoke deeply meaningful experiences and important moments of understanding and realization in players when read aesthetically. To become *literate* in this view of gameplay is to become a player who reads their own game experiences closely, deeply, performatively, and reflectively—with or against the intended or designed experience.

To become an *expert* in this different type of play is to listen to our own experiences as we play and to learn to tell the stories of that play in ways that fully communicate what we have brought back from the journey. In a world of aesthetic players, we are all potential poets and storytellers, and our reflections on that play hold learnings that can be rich life experiences.

Unlike what is implied when we say that describing our play experiences is like giving a list of "mundane choices" (Trefry 2011, 246)—like what cape we equipped, which potion we bought from the shopkeeper, or whether we chose to help a disguised fairy—becoming a literate or even expert aesthetic player means tapping into all the meaningful anticipations of making such choices, the fraught emotional moments of recognizing a betrayal or losing a companion, the connections we make between our game choices and our moral lives, and the up and down beats of suspense, fear, excitement, wonder, regret. When we make a decision in a game, if it is not accompanied by emotions such as this, we have to wonder why. What is our investment in play if it is not to experience such a range of emotions? What is the purpose of play that is not connected to these types of moments? And if play is simply pressing buttons on a controller to make mundane choices—and we know that it is not—then how can we understand it as an aesthetic form at all? Having acknowledged that it is more than simply pressing buttons, then the logical progression of understanding a game leads us from the efferent moments of which buttons to push to the lived, aesthetic experience of why, how, when, and what it all means to us. Given the conclusion that we must go beyond the simple basic efferent literacy of knowing how to perform the actions of a game to teach ourselves to read our gameplay intentionally, as we would read a piece of literature for its deeper pleasures, how can we encourage ourselves and others to become aesthetic players, or, to read our games well?

In chapter 2, when we discuss moving from efferent to close play, we look at the ways in which children are taught to notice their own responses to literature. The realm of children's literature itself is filled with examples of stories that are scaffolded to teach us the ways that language can be used to provoke emotions, ideas, connections, and understanding of deeper and deeper universal themes. We do not start out by reading *Hamlet* or *Ulysses* but move toward them, one book, one poem, or one play at a time, with each new text evoking a new aesthetic experience and a new set of abilities in our reach to become better readers. This assumes, however, that we desire to become better readers. One issue with our analogy to literacy—and literature, in general—is that so many readers (young and old) have very low basic literacy and, therefore, little to no ambition to become better readers of any texts, much less harder-to-parse literary texts or the kind of multimodal texts that games represent.

In reading teacher and author Donalyn Miller's *Reading in the Wild: The Book Whisperer's Keys to Cultivating Lifelong Reading Habits* (2013), she quotes well-known issues around declining reading time for young people and its correlation to performance on standardized reading tests. So, though a student in the twentieth percentile reads books for 0.7 minutes per day, a student in the eightieth percentile reads books for 14.2 minutes per day, and a student in the ninetieth percentile reads for 21.1 minutes per day. At the top of the outcomes, a student in the ninety-eighth percentile reads for 65 minutes per day (D. Miller 2013). We don't have this kind of clear-cut data correlating the performance of game players to standardized tests; however, there is some data to suggest that playing video games two to three times a week can increase scores in math and science as well as in reading (Pasqualotto et al. 2022; Posso 2015). Accepting that the kind of multimodal literacy that games offer is as important as the kind of core literacy skills that reading offers leads us to believe that becoming better aesthetic readers of games may, in fact, encourage the kind of inquisitive, thoughtful, self-driven media consumption that Miller describes in her discussion of what it means to be "wild" or lifelong readers.

Our goals in encouraging the aesthetic reading of games are similar to encouraging the lifelong reading of books. They are to cultivate "well-read" players of games who have an innate love of play and are able to glean from that play the kind of understanding that makes us awake, integrated, healthy, and productive individuals and members of society. The National Endowment for the Arts report "To Read or Not to Read" (Gioia 2007) finds that "regular reading not only boosts the likelihood of an individual's academic and economic success—facts that are not especially surprising—but it also seems to awaken a person's social and civic sense" (6). Adults who consider themselves readers vote in elections, volunteer for charities, and support the arts in greater numbers than their peers who read less. Clearly, developing lifelong reading habits matters not only to the individual but also to society in general. We all benefit when more people read. Again, we do not have similar data to offer for players of games; however, our premise is that as we become more thoughtful, articulate, confident readers of games and other multimodal texts, a similar outcome may be expected. Our reasons for having these expectations lie in the related motivations of "wild readers" and well-read players. The pleasures that drive reading are, as we see in chapter 7, similar to the pleasures that drive play. At the root of these pleasures lies the kind of intellectual and emotional stimulation that promotes learning, growth, and connection to others.

Game designer Chris Bateman has written a series of blog posts on game aesthetics that pull together the design theories from Raph Koster's book *Theory of Fun for Game Design* (2004) and Dan Cook's article "The Chemistry of Game Design" (2007), with the learning theories of neuropsychologists Irving Biederman and Edward Vessel (2006) on perceptual pleasure and the brain. In these posts, Bateman (2012) proposes that video games are rewarding to players specifically because they are *novel* and *richly interpretable* experiences, to use Biederman and Vessel's language. By this, they mean that the complex and changing dramatic experiences of games, like a beautiful vista or a mysterious visual image, provoke brain responses that are "highly preferred" over more mundane experiences (Biederman and Vessel 2006, 252). A core requirement for humanistic pleasures seems to be the act of interpreting new experiences and finding ways to integrate them into our existing context. In this sense, the underlying pleasures of games do not differ that widely from the pleasures of literature, art, film, music, or any other media—or of engagement in life itself. New information lights us up and helps us grow, learn, and enjoy life. When that new information comes in the form of a playful experience, it has the same potential as any other aesthetic form to engage us in meaningful pleasures. And if, as we have described throughout this book, we are attentive to the lived experiences of these moments in games—and in all we do—we can become deeply aesthetic readers of our play and our lives.

There are barriers to becoming a well-read player, however, that include resistance to emotional reflection at both an individual and cultural level. Thinking about and recording aesthetic responses may not come naturally to many players. Understanding this, we were careful to assure players who provided the aesthetic readings shared in chapter 7 that they did not need to worry about their responses being "articulate" or "well written." In our prompt, we consciously gave players permission to reflect on their emotions when recounting play experiences and encouraged them to focus on these feelings as well as what happened in their gameplay. We asked them to describe their play to us like they were describing a dream they had to a friend or writing in a personal journal. We also offered anonymity to those who preferred it, as journaling can be deeply personal. These are just some techniques for giving players permission to engage in aesthetic reading of games. However, becoming a well-read player may require more than individual permission. It may require an entirely new perspective on how we view games as an aesthetic form and how we integrate them into our communities of learning and literacy.

Player-Response Journals

Analyzing, discussing, comparing, negotiating, and appreciating our responses are all interconnected parts of a reflective reading process. As Rosenblatt's (1978) "event" of reading suggests, these reflections are ephemeral and often lost in the next moment of gameplay and the next. Similar to the way we forget a dream upon waking or forget exactly how a moment in a film or a book played out, we often forget the way that a game made us feel once the moment has passed. And, unlike with a film or a book, and because our play event is unique to us, we may not recall those ephemeral feelings even when discussing with others because they may not have even faced the same challenge or met the same characters. There may be moments in a game that are not ever reflected in a button push or a moment of feedback—simply moments of decision or of realization, where the player understands something new, perhaps something about themself, and takes a moment to recognize it privately. These reflective moments are rarely mentioned in game reviews or in discussions about what makes games fun or cool. They are typically ignored in our general understanding of what makes games an important art form. But they are critically important to us as players, and the fact that they are so often ignored in our discussions about games can tend to make players feel that they are unimportant and that we should not mention them. Once we begin to talk about our lived experiences in games with other players, however, we begin to notice them more. It is a positive feedback cycle that allows us to become better readers of games simply by reading them more openly and more often.

There is safety and freedom in the process of opening up emotionally and journaling for oneself without fear or worry about potential judgment for others. The act of reflective journaling is self-therapeutic as it promotes "personal growth and development, intuition and self-expression, problem-solving, stress reduction, health benefits, reflection, and critical thinking" (Hiemstra 2001; Portman 2020, 597). Fullerton (2004) has encouraged the process of having students keep a *game journal* in her playcentric process for more than twenty years, and many of the student responses from chapter 7 come from that community of practice. This private process of recording and reflecting on personal game experiences is an important step to reading games as it allows us to capture the fleeting moments of response that may be otherwise lost.

Journaling is perhaps the best first step to becoming a well-read player because players may feel safe to share their feelings in this private process. But the road to becoming a well-read player may pause here for many players if they are not part of a community that encourages and supports the sharing of responses. If we are to see players engage in a wider community of well-read play—as described by Rosenblatt (1978, 146) when she says that an aesthetic reader "likes to hear others' views," or DeKoven (2013, 112–113) when he describes savoring our play at the "nineteenth hole"—we need to create safe spaces where this kind of sharing is supported.

As discussed in the introduction, reader-response notebooks are already common practices in literature classrooms. A reader-response notebook is where readers record their thoughts, reactions, and reflections on the books or texts they are reading. Often, readers decorate these notebooks with stickers, doodles, and favorite quotations, further personalizing them. Some notebooks are digital and shared with online communities of practice (Kesler 2018). Building on this existing tradition, we suggest *player-response journals* for well-read players to guide and engage on a more personal and subjective level, expressing their opinions, emotions, and connections to game experiences.

As the definition of what a text is expands to include other modalities (Gee 2007; Kesler 2018), player-response journals represent a natural extension for recording reflective responses. After all, keeping a journal is like preserving a time capsule for one's thoughts and experiences. It's a bit like having a conversation with yourself about a game, capturing your evolving understanding. And as mentioned, it can be a therapeutic exercise, helping players gain clarity to foster self-awareness.

Building Caring Communities of Well-Read Players

It can take bravery from players to share their feelings with others. As Ruberg (2017) points out, avid game players are often criticized for caring too deeply about their play. And though the players Ruberg is describing in that statement (hardcore gamers) do not tend to share the kind of emotional responses we are encouraging here, it is clear that the current culture around games is one that does not typically foster inclusivity or tolerance of different styles of play or players. Of course, this culture of intolerance extends beyond games to include discussions of other media, politics, identity, and more. We live in a moment when it is very difficult to propose that anyone should feel safe to expose their innermost emotions around any topic, much less games, where toxicity, online, and offline harassment seem to be at a fever pitch. We propose that this crisis of emotional safety is not a reason to reject the need for sharing our responses to games but rather a reason to double down on its importance in our lives as players and as people. So, given the issues we face, how can we build caring and inclusive communities that invite people to become well-read players?

Our theory inherits its basic humanism from DeKoven's discussion of the *play community*. In DeKoven's vision of the play community, which we must grant came long before the invention of online toxicity, he proclaims optimistically, "We are having fun. We are caring. We are safe with each other" (2013, 13). However, *care theory* suggests that to get to this optimistically safe place, we must scaffold our approach to the creation of "a climate for caring"

(Noddings 2012, 777). Care theory advocates for the use of educational methods that prioritize the development of caring relationships between teachers and students, creating an environment where both academic and personal growth can flourish (Noddings 2003). We can extrapolate on the concept of educational communities of care to suggest that the creation of broader communities for well-read players might require the same scaffolded approach. For example, teaching players to respond to texts in smaller groups first, with mentoring and inclusive support, before encouraging them to engage in larger public forums, such as internet groups.

One common play pattern for games that can create the initial foundations for a safe play community is that of *coplaying*. In coplay, one person is playing and another friend or partner is looking on, commenting, and experiencing the game with them. This type of collaborative play evokes an opportunity for shared experience as two (or more) players discuss and cointerpret each game sequence. As shared in chapter 1, Farber coplayed *Unpacking* with his son, where they discussed and connected the act of unboxing to their recent familial move. When this kind of coplay occurs between parents and children, the children can become experts, reading and responding to the game aloud, narrating and explaining as they play. Or parents can prompt children to think more introspectively about the situations occurring in the game, guiding younger players to become more thoughtful about what they are experiencing. Like the tradition of reading books together, coplaying can be an important aspect of scaffolding young players to become sensitive and open to their emotional responses to a game. Even when siblings, friends, or partners play together, the kind of discussion that coplay provokes can provide an excellent foundation for capturing and developing our responses to play. The most important part about these situations, however, is the safety they provide for speaking aloud about our emotional responses to play. For many players, coplay situations may be the first time they have ever articulated anything beyond their most mundane responses to play. Normalizing this kind of open sharing of emotional responses is a good foundational step in building caring communities of well-read players, and can lead to an opportunity for larger group play, but also for deeper journaling and thoughtful conversation about gameplay.

As we coplay, we may also develop the ability to *play-aloud* about our experiences as they are occurring by simply speaking to a companion about what we are thinking and feeling. This skill holds interesting opportunities for the development of player response and is a well-known technique in user research for games and other experiences known as a *think-aloud*. Jakob Nielsen (2012) of the Nielsen Norman Group explains, "In a thinking aloud test, you ask test participants to use the system while continuously thinking out loud—that is, simply verbalizing their thoughts as they move through the user interface" (para. 4). In game design and game studies, this technique has been adapted to a play-aloud, asking players to verbalize their thoughts and feelings as they play a game. This is a technique that Fullerton (2004, 2024) describes in her book *Game Design Workshop* and has used for many years in her classes and at the Game Innovation Lab to discover how players are responding to the emotional experience goals set by designers. Players are asked to describe what they are seeing, thinking, and feeling about the characters, the situation, what they think their objectives are, and how they are trying to achieve them. Often, when events surprise or move them, they will react with deep emotions during play. In formal user research tests, these play-alouds are often captured on video for review and cataloging by the researchers. But for personal aesthetic readings, we might consider simply recording our play-alouds using a cell phone sitting next to us, or capturing our play with streaming tools. Alternatively, simply speaking aloud while we play can help us mark momentary feelings so that we can write about them later in a journal.

One interesting connection between play-alouds and online gaming communities is the concept of the *let's play* video, a playthrough video where a streamer provides their subjective commentary while they play for an online audience. Most let's play videos focus on the kind of efferent play that we are not interested in here. Streamers will discuss how to work through each level of a game, focusing on exactly which features to use and giving away cheats and secrets. Other let's plays are speedruns, like the *Gone Home* example discussed in chapter 3. Whereas most let's play videos focus on providing humor and efferent information about games, a few do touch on the kind of emotional response that we might consider to be an aesthetic reading, or at least an introspective reading. In Greg Miller's "Quietest Let's Play Ever—Kinda Funny Plays *That Dragon, Cancer*," Miller comments only briefly on his play experience, letting his facial expressions provide emotional commentary as he plays the game. In the end, he shares his thoughts about the story being "one of those situations that you hope you never have to be in: losing a child, having to make these kinds of decisions, having to walk through these kinds of things. But video games offer the chance to hop in someone else's shoes, and maybe get a little perspective on your own life through the trials and tribulations of others" (Kinda Funny Games 2016, 55:05). Like *That Dragon, Cancer*, *Walden, a game* engenders an experience that is perhaps not well suited to a typical let's play. But when players do open up about their emotional responses, their let's plays can be quite moving. One streamer becomes upset when she realizes that Thoreau's brother had died during her playthrough, saying, "I guess Henry secluded himself to maybe face his demons. So my view on Henry has changed a bit. I just thought he was doing this as an experiment, as a scientist, but that's not the case. So he didn't just come to do an experiment; he came to get away. Because he lost his brother, and Emerson lost his son, and we lost Emerson, in a sense. We lost Ellen. This just got really depressing." (SinaeAzule 2017, 1:10). The streamer goes on to say that this emotional response makes the game much more interesting to her and commits to doing the abolitionist quests in the game, saying that the sense of purpose in helping fugitives from slavery might have been another reason for Thoreau's time in the woods. Her decision to transform Thoreau's personal tragedies into activist passion in her gameplay shows a fascinating potential for aesthetic reading of games to help players form the same kind of intellectual connections in their own lives.

Whether in private coplay settings or in more public forums like let's play videos, the act of playing aloud is related to the traditional *read-aloud* technique for books, which is used to encourage social reflective literacy skills for written texts. In a read-aloud, there is a back-and-forth exchange between an adult and a child, or children, as they read passages out loud together and discuss them. Read-alouds have the purpose of promoting "collective meaning-making . . . opportunities for children to become immersed in a literature experience as they listen and respond to book events in ways that are meaningful for them, not events in which the children's only role is as a passive audience" (Sanden et al. 2021, 63–64). For this to occur, the reader needs to trust that the person or persons they are reading to are caring people who foreground compassion and support for their experience and expression of ideas.

In Lawrence Sipe's (2008) book *Storytime: Young Children's Literary Understanding in the Classroom*, five categories of responses to texts are shared: analytical, intertextual, personal, transparent, and performative. He recommends that adults pause at sections when reading aloud, asking children to then make inferences into narrative gaps and to respond to situations and themes. We might make the same suggestion for coplaying and play-alouds. What would a coplay or let's play look like if we paused the game to respond to difficult emotional moments or make connections between characters, situations, and gameplay? It might look like the quiet, contemplative examples of let's plays from *That Dragon, Cancer* and *Walden*, or it might look like the interlude scenes from the *Life Is Strange* series discussed in chapter 4. As they play, players might share aesthetic responses to the game, perhaps connecting to their own lives in the way that we saw in the player journals shared in chapter 7. Similar to Sipe's suggestions for reading books with children, adult coplayers can pause a game in sections to offer responses that connect to Sipe's five categories. Of course, this suggestion doesn't have to be restricted to children and adults—plenty of couples play together, as do friends, coworkers, and other groups. Playing together is a natural way to bring out conversation about what we are experiencing.

Once we have built the kind of reflection skills that make us an articulate reader of games, whether by journaling or playing aloud, we will have the foundation that we need to participate in a broader community of well-read players. For many book readers, *book clubs* are a place that fosters a sense of community and intellectual stimulation where they can deepen their appreciation for the written word. Book clubs may be formed by individuals or by a community organization that selects a specific title to read within a defined time frame. Clubs then convene to explore the intricacies of chosen works, exchange thoughts, unpack experiences, and share interpretations and opinions. These discussions often transcend mere analysis of plot and characters, delving into the broader themes, symbolism, and cultural context of the book. These meetings also allow participants to practice the art of dialogue with others, either face to face, via video conference, or sometimes in an online forum. In a world where social media has taught us to simply pontificate our ideas, book clubs teach us to listen and learn from others, to put forth our ideas in dialogue with others—very different from the short, decontextualized posts found on messaging apps like X (formerly Twitter) or TikTok. Whether in person or virtual, book clubs are meant to be safe spaces where the magic of storytelling becomes a shared, social experience.

Some newer works of literary fiction include discussion guides for book clubs. Websites like Goodreads also may include discussion prompts shared by community members to be used at book clubs. (Goodreads is currently owned by Amazon, originally just a bookseller.) Celebrities and online influencers have created book clubs, too, which extend their brands by building communities around reading. Oprah Winfrey and Reese Witherspoon recommend literary works to their respective followers; in bookshops, their book club logos are affixed on covers, adding an element of celebrity cache, as these are considered curated, handpicked titles. An example of reader-response discussion questions from the Oprah Winfrey Book Club include, "How did [the book] impact you? Do you think you'll remember it in a few months or years?" (Nicolaou 2020, para. 4).

The idea of bringing book clubs into classrooms was developed in the 1990s by scholar Taffy E. Raphael "to integrate reading, writing, student-led discussion groups, whole-class discussion, and instruction" (Raphael and McMahon 1994, 102). Reader-response theory flourishes when the role of the reader in a reader-text relationship is a part of social group discussions (McMahon and Raphael 1997). At the time, book clubs in classrooms represented a shift from teaching reading as a solitary act to including shared, social experiences. More than simply unpacking and discussing texts aloud in groups, book clubs put *social constructivism* into action, the learning theory guided by play, as learners actively construct knowledge, language, and cultural understanding through collaboration with others (Vygotsky 1967, 1978).

What could these kinds of safe, discussion-based communities lend to the experience of playing games? Beyond written texts, it can be rare for book club–style discussion prompts to be created for player communities. Even in some game studies programs, courses or workshops presented as "book clubs for video games" are often still focused on the more efferent aspects of gameplay rather than aesthetic responses. For example, in Professor José Zagal's Critical

Game Studies class at the University of Utah, which he shared with us as an example of a "book club for video games," the kinds of discussion prompts include "What kinds of decisions must the player make from moment to moment? How are those decisions interesting from a player's perspective? In what way are those decisions tactical?" Zagal, whose Well Played essay we discussed in chapter 3, understands that these are not the kind of prompts that will provoke deep examination from a humanities or aesthetic perspective. The goals of his one-credit seminar center more on developing systems literacy for his game students rather than reading games from the perspective we are proposing here. Even USC Games, where Fullerton teaches, for years held a Game Deconstruction Salon where the same kinds of systems-focused questions were asked and discussed. It is rare to find the kind of "book club for video games" that we are proposing, even in our own institutions and social groups.

What would such a group look like? For example, if the coplayers or let's play streamers described above addressed questions similar to those posed by the Oprah Winfrey Book Club quoted above: "How did [the game] impact you? Do you think you'll remember it in a few months or years?" Or if these same players addressed a prompt similar to the one we gave to our community when seeking game journal submissions: "What resonated with you as you played the game? Think about a moment of gameplay that was emotionally moving and tell us about it. Focus on the emotions, what happened, describe it as you might describe a dream to a friend, or as you might write in a personal journal." These kinds of questions would certainly elicit a different response than questions about player decisions and tactics. Perhaps publishers of games could bundle player-response questions as ancillary materials on platforms like Steam or Discord. What would a book club on *The Last of Us* (Naughty Dog 2013) look like if it was led by Neil Druckmann, copresident of its developer, and Bruce Straley, the creative director? Or if communities posted questions on Discord or Twitch to engage players in reflective play? Who are the Reese Witherspoon or Oprah Winfrey influencers who can drive gaming communities toward an online culture of well-read players? How would a game writer like Rhianna Pratchett, the writer of *Lost Words*, engage well-read adolescent players through a book club–like discussion? What would it be like if players were given a journal like Izzy was given by her grandmother, with the same prompt: "A writer writes." Could that journal also include book club–like questions for players separated by chapter, like the game? The dynamics of small, safe group video game book clubs provide a promising potential model for sharing emotional responses and for growing our understanding of games as an aesthetic form.

Creating safe places for such discussions is not as simple as it might seem. Many online gaming communities tend to devolve into unsafe and potentially toxic spaces. Sensitive let's plays like the ones quoted above are the exception, not the rule. Much of online gamer culture cultivates a hardcore, efferent approach to game fandom, protecting itself from the kind of inclusive and open sharing we suggest. Power and control of these spaces is hotly contested by fans who do not want games to deviate from the kind of action-focused content they enjoy. Alternative and narrative play is derided, and players who enjoy this kind of play, as well as developers who make it, can be harassed in the extreme. Finding a safe environment to develop our own personal responses to games rather than being co-opted by the opinions and prejudices of others is a difficult task to say the least. But it is the project of this book to insist that doing so is the only way to become a fully realized player of games, an aesthetic reader of games, and to understand and appreciate the holistic value of play in our lives as humans. The question of how to break the cycle of player-policed dehumanization of play in our culture is a difficult one, to which there is no easy answer. Our participation in play begins in childhood, as do our expectations about what it means to be a player of games. If we are not given permission and skills to articulate our feelings about that play openly as we grow, we are likely to set those feelings aside and focus only on the efferent nature of the experience. If, however, we can build the foundations of a well-read game appreciation into our lives and growth, we may find ways to rebalance the current status of gamer culture, away from protective toxicity and toward a more open sharing of all the experiences that games can offer.

One possibility for breaking the cycle might be to invite games into *literature circles*, a more gamelike form of the book club format that shares the common goal of fostering a love for reading and the facilitation of meaningful discussions through role-play. Literature circles have gamelike roles for participants to take on, such as discussion leader, summarizer, connector, or illustrator. Each contributor is tasked with bringing a unique perspective to the group dialogue. These roles serve to support Socratic seminars, a form of collaborative discussion that encourages critical thinking and deep exploration of a topic or text. Named after the Greek philosopher Socrates, this method involves participants engaging in open-ended dialogue, posing questions, and responding to one another's ideas. The goal, like a book club, is to collectively explore and gain a deeper understanding of a particular text; however, in this case, each member plays a different part in the discussion. The playfully formal aspect of this type of discussion is meant to normalize a culture of safe and thoughtful sharing for participants who may not yet have the skills to engage in open-ended dialogue. Setting these kinds of boundaries on the sharing process can build the kind of foundational skills that many young people have not acquired in regard to their gameplay. As discussed earlier, establishing a "climate for caring" for authentic and empathetic responses to blossom is critical (Noddings 2012, 777). Framing expectations and norms before discussions begin can help establish a culture for safe and thoughtful sharing, unlike what we see in many gamer forums.

As it happens, Farber's son regularly takes part in literature circles in his school. For instance, he and his classmates annotate Arthur

Miller's (1953) play *The Crucible* with sticky notes and highlighter markers and then take part in student-led Socratic seminars guided by reader-response questions. After reading aloud and enacting parts of the play where they call upon their own emotions and experiences when interpreting character motivations, they consider the Salem witch crisis as an allegory for the Red Scare in the 1950s. Guided discussions include modern-day "witch hunts," such as persecutions that affect youth culture: from politics to gender identity. The circle also discussed the 1996 film adaptation starring Daniel Day-Lewis and Winona Ryder, comparing it to the play. Similarly, when Farber was a history teacher, *The Crucible* was part of his lessons. In addition to Miller's theatrical work, he used the social deduction card game *One Night Ultimate Werewolf* (Bezier Games 2014) to experientially teach witch hunts. After players lied, bluffed, and accused one another of being werewolves, he asked how they felt about being falsely accused to draw out player readings of the experience. Some responded by expressing their feelings of being labeled by peers and how rumormongering affected them. Other games that could be used in a group like this are social deduction party card games Mafia and Assassin, as well as *Among Us* (Innersloth 2018), the popular multiplayer video game about rooting out imposters on a sabotaged spaceship. All of these might be paired with *The Crucible* to elicit personal and introspective responses to both the written and playable texts.

The practice of pairing different forms of texts is actually a common approach in literacy instruction dating back to the mid-1990s. Although many definitions exist, paired texts can be defined as any two texts that are "conceptually related in some way" by genre, topic, or theme (Ciecierski and Bintz 2016, 33). In the example above, false accusation is felt in social deduction games that create a bit of background knowledge to be brought to Miller's play. Farber and Erekson (2023) suggest this approach for children's librarians, thematically pairing the game *Lost Words* with Ali Benjamin's (2015) novel *The*

Thing about Jellyfish. Both the game and the book are based on the hero's journey and incorporate the theme of grief, experiences players and readers may have encountered in their real lives. The game can be invited into literature circles with the novel, where multiple perspectives and interpretations can then be shared (Farber and Erekson 2023).

Games such as these can be a kind of virtual field trip experience that can create background knowledge for appreciating difficult written texts. After all, it is clearly not safe to accuse and rumormonger about anyone, nor would it be possible to simulate grief realistically. We must realize, however, that not all games are safe for all players. In *Repairing Play: A Black Phenomenology* (2023), scholar Aaron Trammell argues that white European philosophers of play, many of whom we cover in this book, ignore the possibility that what is playful for some can be traumatic to Black, Indigenous, and people of color (BIPOC) communities. For instance, games of tag, capture the flag, and hide-and-seek are not positive experiences for some, as these games also have historical associations with violence. Trammell (2023) recommends recentering Black experiences and decolonizing play, as much of play involves power dynamics. He writes, "A radical phenomenology of play centers on the moments when play is painful (as opposed to pleasurable) to recenter the BIPOC narratives that focus on the traumatic and violent aspects of games and play" (Trammel 2023, 11). When building caring spaces for reflective players, inclusivity is essential, as are communities that are supportive. To become well-read players, it is as important to recognize when our play may be hurtful or harmful to ourselves or others and to have a safe space to discuss and unpack that play in ways that will help us grow and learn. This is one reason why the creation of these kinds of caring communities for well-read play is such a critical topic for us.

Libraries may be good first venues for the creation of game-based literature circles or book clubs as potentially safe in-person spaces for patrons to meet and discuss games. Other informal learning communities, such as museums and literacy organizations like the National Writing Project, the National Council of Teachers of English, and International Literacy Association, could curate and moderate group discussions, too. Our own work has included classroom discussions as well as informal learning situations. The lessons we created for *Walden, a game EDU* (Fullerton and USC Game Innovation Lab, 2023) form an ecosystem that pairs the game with Henry David Thoreau's book and other writings—and with the players' lives. Lessons include open-ended discussion prompts that can be used in literature circles as well as an in-game journal that can be exported for additional notetaking. Players respond to the game *and* Thoreau's written text, which is embedded in the game itself. Questions students are asked include "Do you agree with Thoreau's ideas around self-reliance and his critique of materialism? What examples of materialism do you see in the society around you?" (Fullerton et al. 2022, 5). Student responses to these questions, asked after playing the game and reading sections of the text, include comments such as "I think I agree with Thoreau's critique, and it made me realize that we only need the essentials in life. I think I see things in life that we do not need such as products or things we like that other people like, so we follow that pattern in society. I think this game and philosophy showed me how to resist materialism." Another student responded: "I believe in certain aspects of Thoreau's idea. I believe the competition for who has the best or newest of everything is not good, but new medicines and other things that do good are important. Competition is the drive for humans to make good things. I think that a modern example of materialism could be technology. Resisting it is not always up to me, because ultimately it is my parents who decide whether I get a new phone or laptop. It is my choice to be upset about it or not, and I will admit, when I have the oldest phone, or a different type of computer than my peers, it bothers me more than it should." These kinds of responses are not specific to the game, obviously, but the student's interest and openness to discussing Thoreau's philosophy, according to their teacher, is related to the fact that they were able to play the philosophy themselves in the game and respond to it at a greater level of authenticity than if they had simply read the assigned text.

Paul Darvasi and Farber led the writing of another set of game-based lessons around the thematic elements of *Edith Finch.* These lessons, created for the iThrive Games Foundation (iThrive Curriculum 2021), included activities such as Harkness discussions, which are similar to Socratic seminars in literature circles. This approach typically involves students sitting in an oval—round and facing inward, much like a literature circle—sharing in a role-based environment. In this case, roles included a moderator, a timekeeper, a notetaker, and a researcher. Harkness discussion prompts for *Edith Finch* ranged from "What is the Finch family curse? Is it really a curse?" to "Edith says that her mother, Dawn, is 'very good at keeping secrets.' Do you think secrets should be kept within families? Do you think Dawn's secrets did more harm or good? Should families be completely transparent with each other? Why or why not?" (Darvasi and Farber 2021, 1). Students are able to share their own experiences with familial secrets as they broach the subject in discussion. In an iThrive Games promotional video about the *Edith Finch* lessons, a student comments, "What I learned about myself is [that] I should start journaling more. I already liked to write, but ever since we started playing the game, I started journaling again and taking it a little more seriously" (iThrive Games 2019, 0:50). Interestingly, player journals were not part of these lessons, though the narrative in the game unfolds in notes and journal entries. Perhaps the ecosystem of in-game journals, alongside group discussions, led this player to take up her own journaling.

As James Paul Gee (2003) points out in the *self-knowledge principle*, the experiences offered by gameplay can inform our understanding of ideas but also of ourselves and our abilities. He advocates for gameplay that is "constructed in such a way that learners learn not only about the domain but about themselves and their current and potential capacities" (208). In the conclusion of *What Video Games Have to Teach Us about Learning and Literacy* (2003), Gee ruminates on how people "read" video games, "what meanings they make from them," wondering about a future in which there will be "some 'canonical' games, games that lend themselves powerfully to elevating the aspirations and imaginings of all people for better and more just worlds. These may be new aspirations and imaginings or ones that fill old visions with new meanings and hope" (204–205).

We very much agree that gameplay can help elevate the aspirations and imaginings of players, but to reach this ideal, we must be brave and open enough to engage with games in the same way that we (hopefully) engage with life and with more familiar types of expressive texts. That is, as part of a process of reflection and interpretation that helps us to better understand ourselves, others, and the world. Engaging with games as a well-read player means questioning our assumptions about what games are, what roles they can play in our lives, and what expectations we should have for them as an aesthetic form. And, as we have seen, reading games aesthetically relies on being open to the sensitivity of our responses, as well as an ability to challenge the common assumptions about play and what it can mean to us. This may mean building new, inclusive communities of play where we are safe and free enough to read games emotionally and truthfully. When we read games, we must be able to open ourselves up to bringing our "baggage," as Rosenblatt calls it. This includes all our past experiences, our faults and prejudices, as well as our hopes and aspirations. If each new game we play can bring something new to our understanding of ourselves and the world, then becoming a well-read player will help us to become better people, as well as better players. Each new reading becomes a part of our personal journeys of meaning and learning that help us to recommit ourselves to the world and to leading better, more reflective lives.

Conclusion

As we come to the close of our discussion, we would like to revisit the words of Sophia Ouellette, the fifteen-year-old *Journey* player that we quote in our introduction. Sophia speaks about her experience of playing this game with her father, who was himself dying of cancer. Sophia wisely articulates the "profound connection" that she and her father found with others and with each other as they made their way through this difficult time while playing the game. Reflecting on her experience in *Journey* gave Sophia a way to write about what she was feeling about her father's death and the courage to turn her emotions into a creative expression that went on to touch the developers and many others with whom they shared the story. "It's this beautiful example of the End," Sophia says, "and that it doesn't have to be a bad thing. . . . I realized this journey within the game, it reflected the journey I was going on with my dad." This reading is such a mature and touching example of what it means for us to be a well-read player that it is stunning that it comes from such a young person, but one who was able to listen clearly as she played to Rosenblatt's "shimmering interplay of meanings, associations, feeling-tones" (Rosenblatt 1978, 54).

We began this book by situating our idea of player response in the work of Rosenblatt and Dewey, whose writings on the phenomenological experiences of art and literature have been central to the development of emotionally aware readers for decades. The idea that literature, specifically, and the arts, more generally, are experiences that allow us to develop and understand our own emotional literacy is critical to our ultimate goal with this book. That is, to establish a foundation for talking about our experiences with games, and through that dialogue, to grow and learn from these experiences in ways that make us better players, better people, and more able to engage with the complex situations that face us as citizens of today's world. For both Dewey and Rosenblatt, the purpose of reading is to understand complex life situations, and the work of art exists as a "process of becoming . . . across the experiences of readers" (Faust 2000, 18). That process of becoming is a "continually mediated process in which social context provides constraints that limit, channel, and enable readers' ways of thinking about, talking about, and representing the meaning they impute to written signs" (Faust 2000 quoting Smagorinsky and O'Donnell-Allen 1998, 18). This social process, which we see as integral to our concept of safe, inclusive communities of well-read games, holds the potential to build foundational skills not only in multimodal literacy but also in social and emotional awareness and civic consciousness.

As we have seen, the process of becoming such a reader of games begins with learning to read games closely and deeply. Becoming thoughtful, deliberate readers of what happens when we play (as illustrated in figure 0.2 in the introduction), means that we are sensitive to and acknowledge not only the efferent aspects of our play but the emotional and aesthetic aspects of these experiences as well. Becoming aware of this metaprocess of play, and being able to articulate that experience is, as Dewey (1934) put it, the actual "work" of art. He writes, "a beholder must *create* [their] own experience" (40). And that creation of an experience is not just an individual process. It is one that is part of the intertextual experience of reading, discussing, modifying, rereading, and building ideas described in chapter 8, that is, in Rosenblatt's view, "the essence of the democratic process" (Faust 2000, 28).

When we build these foundational skills in close and deep reading of play, we are preparing to perform more complex types of social and emotional play—in games and in life. But as we have seen, this performance requires the safety of private play as well as a supportive and inclusive community of play. Becoming part of such a community of play lies at the heart of DeKoven's philosophy. And building such a care community takes vision and structure, whether that be in small, private communities or more elaborate public communities. To perform the kinds of rich emotional play that can truly transform us, we need the safety to be able to sense and acknowledge our own feelings in play, to stop playing, or to change the game when we don't feel safe any longer. We also need the social and emotional skills to identify our feelings and to be able to listen to them more clearly. When we are aware of our own emotions, we need to be able to listen to those of others as well. Listening to the thoughts of others, sharing our own thoughts, and building on these thoughts together as we read the games we play are all part of the core skills of perspective-taking and understanding that allow us to approach one another with compassion and empathy.

When we speak of twenty-first-century skills today, we often lead with the idea that systems thinking should be seen as the most important skill that can be taken away from our play of games. But surely, that is only one aspect of what we can learn from games. The social and emotional learning that we get from reading games as aesthetic experiences, and the deep catharsis that is possible from performing and participating in these emotionally rich experiences, is as important as what we might learn from inhabiting a game only from the perspective of its systems. Our lives are made up of systems, but that is not all they are made up of. Similarly, our written literature and other forms of storytelling and expression also consist of underlying systems, such as language itself or visual and aural systems, but that is not all or even most of what we can learn from them. Too narrow a focus on what an experience like gameplay offers can lead us to misunderstand its true potential.

To be frank, our understanding of literature sometimes suffers from the same paucity of vision as that of games. Many of us may have learned in school to read literature as a kind of quest for the facts of the text. We may have been taught to critique the text only from the point of view of the author. We are taught to search for what they were trying to express rather than what we evoked when we imagined and lived the text ourselves. Reader response, even in today's classrooms, is often twisted to deny readers their own place in the process of creation. But games don't need to suffer this problem; they are already understood to be "interactive" experiences. Given that open door, we can simply step through to a realm of player response where that interactivity is acknowledged to extend to the aesthetic experience as well as the systemic. The benefits of such a step are clear.

Well-read players possess both the multimodal literacy skills and the social and emotional skills that will make them uniquely equipped to participate in today's complex societies. In the same manner that approaching reading and literature as a creative adventure are understood to prepare us for the unfinished nature of life experiences, so too can our theory of player response and the well-read game prepare us for these same situations. We have seen in the player readings throughout this book that the kinds of readings players do when they are open to claiming the rewards of player response are as deep as we might expect from any traditional form of literature or expression. They are also as broad as we might expect, spanning responses of growth and grief, love and loss, freedom and belongingness. The players who contributed their responses to this book have also spanned from high school students to older professionals. They come from cultures across the world, including those in Asia, Europe, and the United States. They are of a spectrum of genders and sexual identities, as well as a spectrum of socioeconomic backgrounds. The thing they have in common is that they are all so moved by their experiences of games that they make the effort to read those experiences aesthetically. And, when they feel safe and supported to do so, they are open to sharing those experiences with other readers.

What do we bring back with us when we go on the journey to become a well-read player of games? Like all journeys, that answer will be different for each player of each game each time that they play. When Fullerton was a child, her parents brought home a mysterious black and white box from Sears, Roebuck and Co. Her father carefully hooked it up to their Zenith television with a fascinating A/B switch that allowed the television to change back and forth from telling stories to making them. Fullerton remembers the experience vividly, her first steps to becoming a well-read player:

> My sister and I lay on the floor close to the screen and pressed "Start game." The ball was served. It was square, but even so, I knew it was a ball by how it moved. I twirled the knob on the right and my paddle moved into position, just below position, really, so that I could move it as I hit the ball, giving it a bit of English on the return. The ball sailed away toward my sister's side of the court. She hit it back. Back and forth, again and again. We were in a groove. We were playing well together. No one was poking or crying. The comforting bleeps and bloops accompanied our sudden laughs at the ups and downs of the game. It was magic. Our parents were equally entranced by the glowing, moving square on the screen that represented something real, imaginary, and impossible all at once.

DeKoven (2013) describes another game of ping-pong in the *Well-Played Game*, in which two players are searching for what it means to play together well. The players realize that one of them is more skilled than the other and so create a way to even the playing field. Then they realize that eventually one of them will win, even though winning is not the goal of their search for a well-played game. So, they decide to play without scoring to see if that helps. Just volleying back and forth, playing gently with each other, trying to keep the volley going as long as possible. They begin to use the word "we" instead of "I" when they refer to how their play is going: "We seem to be getting the feel of it! . . . I can sense the game, I can sense you, I can sense the way we're playing it together. And I love it. I love being this way. I love doing this thing, playing this game with you" (DeKoven 2013, 29). The players have found a way to play the game well together. Before they find this groove, though, there are some false starts. They are distracted by the innate assumption that winning is the goal of the game, and that the game is the arbiter of the experience. "The old values are still too strong for me to play with," DeKoven laments, "their hold is too strong" (28).

We face a similar challenge in beginning the journey to become a well-played reader of games. The assumed values of games as systems of adjudication over our efforts and experiences are strongly held. Our ephemeral moments of aesthetic play are buried under discussions of how platforming controls feel or how many frames per second the graphics are playing at. Even by discussions of how the system is designed. But there are fleeting moments where we are feeling and playing and being with and in the game that provoke the kind of reflective play experiences that we should be seeking, not ignoring. Like any good hero on the journey of trials, we may have first taken a wrong path, listened to the wrong advice, or taken up with the wrong allies. We are at the midpoint now, where we must reconsider why we are going on this journey at all. What we need, versus what we think we want. It is time to look back at those experiences we have all had in play, the ones that we cannot forget but don't talk about with others. It is time to understand what the real outcome of our journey could be. We should be cherishing those beautiful, reflective experiences like jewels, holding them up and saying, "I found something in this game. I have discovered something. Something happened to me, it changed me, and I need to tell you about it." As called for in the introduction to this book, we should be coming back from our journeys in games holding those precious gems of experience close until we can write about it or tell someone about it, until we can bring it safely back with us into the world like the elixir of our hero's journey.

Several years ago, Farber and his son, six years old at the time, played *Never Alone* together in cooperative mode. His son played the main protagonist, Nuna, whereas Farber assisted as the Arctic Fox. The game, also described in chapter 7, is a narrative platformer based on an Iñupiaq Alaska Native folktale. It was a strange feeling for Farber as a parent because the game's asymmetrical mechanics endowed his son with unique abilities. Only Nuna could ascend ladders, push blocks, and toss a bola weapon into the sky. The Arctic Fox has different abilities, such as leaping across chasms, climbing ice walls, and shimmying into tight spaces. As a result, the game models the importance of interdependence, telling a hero's journey from the point of view of a young child and their animal ally. Farber journaled his son's emotional response when the Arctic Fox, who had been helping him all along, is unexpectedly killed by the Manslayer:

> For my son, it is the first time he experiences death and loss in a video game that seems permanent. I know this is the death and rebirth part of the hero's journey cycle, having played the game once before in single-player mode. But he is visibly upset. "Is Fox really dead?" he asks. I encourage him to keep playing to find out. I know Fox does return later, transformed as a spirit. I think about how this experience is preparing him for his life's journey when he will encounter death and loss. Am I his Arctic Fox? When I am gone, will he be okay?

The journey of writing this book has connected us with the experiences of many players—our own, one another's, and those of our extended community of play. With each new reading we discover a new gem of experience. Some are difficult, some are joyful, and all are important parts of what it means to be a playful human. We hope that taking this journey with us has returned you a bit changed to the world, ready perhaps to play with an aesthetic attitude, to seek more than the efferent in your understanding of games. What's at stake for the world of play, we believe, is the potential of this aesthetic form to be understood as a measure not of individual success, victory, or achievement, but rather a path to wholeness, wellness, and a collective building of experience that sit at the heart of what it means to be human. Who knows, but if we are able to become better readers of games, perhaps we will also be able to become better "players" of literature and of life. Imagine a world where playfulness gives us all permission to articulate our lived experiences—not only in the realm of the aesthetic but beyond. This would truly be a wonderland. As Lewis Carroll's (1865) Alice responded, returning from her own journey there:

> "Oh, I've had such a curious dream!" said Alice, and she told her sister, as well as she could remember them, all these strange Adventures of hers that you have just been reading about. (113)

References

Alberti, John. 2008. "The Game of Reading and Writing: How Video Games Reframe Our Understanding of Literacy." *Computers and Composition* 25 (3): 258–269.

Barthes, Roland. 1970. *S/Z*. New York: Hill and Wang.

———. 1977. "The Death of the Author." In *Image, Music, Text*, translated and edited by Stephen Heath, 153. New York: Hill and Wang.

Bateman, Chris. 2012. "Implicit Game Aesthetics (4): Cook's Chemistry." *International Hobo* (blog). May 9, 2012. https://blog.ihobo.com/2012/05/implicit-game-aesthetics-4-cooks-chemistry.html.

Beltrán, Whitney "Strix." 2012. "Yearning for the Hero Within: Live Action Role-Playing as Engagement with Mythical Archetypes." In *Wyrd Con Companion 2012*, edited by Sarah Lynne Bowman and Aaron Vanek, 91–98. Los Angeles: Wyrd Con.

Benjamin, Ali. 2015. *The Thing about Jellyfish*. Boston: Little, Brown.

Biederman, Irving, and Edward Vessel. 2006. "Perceptual Pleasure and the Brain." *American Scientist* 94 (3): 247–253.

Bishop, Rudine Sims. 1990. "Mirrors, Windows, and Sliding Glass Doors." *Perspectives* 1 (3): ix–xi.

Block, Bruce A. 2008. *The Visual Story: Creating the Visual Structure of Film, TV, and Digital Media*. 2nd ed. Amsterdam: Focal Press/Elsevier.

Bohman-Kalaja, Kimberly. 2007. *Reading Games: An Aesthetics of Play in Flann O'Brien Samuel Beckett and Georges Perec*. Champaign, IL: Dalkey Archive Press.

Bogost, Ian. 2007. *Persuasive Games: The Expressive Power of Videogames*. Cambridge, MA: MIT Press.

Bordwell, David. 1989. *Making Meaning: Inference and Rhetoric in the Interpretation of Cinema*. Cambridge, MA: Harvard University Press.

Bowman, Sarah Lynne. 2015. "Bleed: The Spillover between Player and Character." March 2, 2015. Nordic Larp. https://nordiclarp.org/2015/03/02/bleed-the-spillover-between-player-and-character/.

———. 2018. "Immersion and Shared Imagination in Role-Playing Games." In *Role-Playing Game Studies: Transmedia Foundations*, edited by José P. Zagal and Sebastian Deterding, 379–394. New York: Routledge.

Brad. 2010. "Red Dead Redemption—Bird People Glitch." YouTube video, 2:07. May 23, 2010. https://www.youtube.com/watch?v=kYdCvN-ukRY.

Brand, Stewart. 1976. "Theory of Game Change." In New Games Foundation 1976, 137–140.

Bruner, Jerome S. 1966. *Toward a Theory of Instruction*. Cambridge, MA: Belknap Press.

Caillois, Roger. 1958. *Man, Play and Games*. Urbana: University of Illinois Press.

Campbell, Joseph. 1949. *The Hero with a Thousand Faces*. Novato, CA: New World Library.

Carroll, Lewis. (1865) 1931. *Alice's Adventures in Wonderland*. New York: Three Sirens Press.

———. (1871) 1931. *Through the Looking Glass*. New York: Three Sirens Press.

Charles, Alec. 2009. "Playing with One's Self: Notions of Subjectivity and Agency in Digital Games." *Eludamos* 3 (2): 280–294.

Ciecierski, Lisa, and William Bintz. 2016. "Paired Texts: A Way into the Content Area." *Middle School Journal* 47 (4): 32–44.

Conrad, Joseph. 1899. *"Heart of Darkness." Blackwoods Magazine*.

Cook, Daniel. 2007. "The Chemistry of Game Design." Game Developer. July 19, 2007. https://www.gamedeveloper.com/design/the-chemistry-of-game-design.

Cortez, Arturo, Ashieda McKoy, and José Ramón Lizárraga. 2022. "The Future of Young Blacktivism: Aesthetics and Practices of Speculative Activism in Video Game Play." *Journal of Futures Studies* 26 (3): 53–70.

Crawford, Chris. 2000. *Understanding Interactivity*. San Francisco: Erasmatzz.

Critical Distance. n.d. "Mission Statement." Accessed June 16, 2024. https://www.critical-distance.com/about/.

Cronin, Mariam Karis. 2014. "The Common Core of Literacy and Literature." *English Journal* 103 (4): 46–52.

Csíkszentmihályi, Mihály. 1990. *Flow: The Psychology of Optimal Experience*. New York: Harper and Row.

Darvasi, Paul, and Matthew Farber. 2021. "Possible Museum of Me Harkness Prompts." Google Docs. https://docs.google.com/document/d/18mN31MR9Q-rdskF3i-XNwTVK-pjsMDxYMnd-OtVth-4/edit.

Davidson, Drew, ed. 2011. *Well Played 3.0: Video Games, Value and Meaning*. Pittsburgh: ETC Press.

DeKoven, Bernie. 1978. *The Well-Played Game: A Player's Philosophy*. Anchor Books. Garden City, NY: Anchor Press.

———. 2013. *The Well-Played Game: A Player's Philosophy*. Cambridge, MA: MIT Press.

Dewey, John. 1934. *Art As Experience*. New York: Minton Balch.

Dykehouse, Reannon. 2017. "Gaming for Meaning: Video Games and Evolving Reader Response." MA thesis, Northern Michigan University. https://commons.nmu.edu/theses/132.

Eliot, T. S. 1932. *Selected Essays: 1917–1932*. New York: Harcourt, Brace and Company.

Farber, Matthew. 2018. *Game-Based Learning in Action: How an Expert Affinity Group Teaches with Games*. New York: Peter Lang.

Farber, Matthew, and James Erekson. 2023. "Beyond the Page: Pairing Children's Literature with Video Games." *Children and Libraries* 21 (1): 7–14.

Farber, Matthew, and Karen Schrier. 2021. "Beyond Winning: A Situational Analysis of Two Digital Autobiographical Games." *Game Studies* 21, no. 4 (December). https://gamestudies.org/2104/articles/farber_schrier.

Faust, Mark. 2000. "Reconstructing Familiar Metaphors: John Dewey and Louise Rosenblatt on Literary Art as Experience." *Research in the Teaching of English* 35, no. 1 (August): 9–34.

Feldman, Lee. 2018. "Player-Response: On the Nature of Interactive Narratives as Literature." MA thesis, Chapman University. https://doi.org/10.36837/chapman.000031.

Fernández-Vara, Clara. 2019. *Introduction to Game Analysis*. 2nd ed. New York: Routledge.

Fiske, John. 1987. *Television Culture*. London: Routledge.

Fitzhugh, Louise. 1964. *Harriet the Spy*. New York: Yearling.

Fitzgerald, F. Scott. 1925. *The Great Gatsby*. New York: Signet.

Flynn, Elizabeth A. 2007. "Louise Rosenblatt and the Ethical Turn in Literary Theory." *College English* 70 (1): 52–69.

Fullerton, Tracy. (2004) 2024. *Game Design Workshop: A Playcentric Approach to Creating Innovative Games*. 5th ed. Boca Raton, FL: CRC Press.

———. 2017. "Keynote: Games of Life: Exploring the Arts and Humanities Through Play." Games for Change Festival. YouTube video, 29:29. September 11, 2017. https://www.youtube.com/watch?v=CjD_xGKUd0M.

———. 2018. "Keynote: Three Miles an Hour: Designing Games for the Speed of Thought." Meaningful Play Conference. Michigan State University, October 11, 2018.

Fullerton, Tracy, Matthew Farber, and Matthew Coopilton. 2022. "Walden, a game EDU—Lesson: Self-Reliance." Tracy Fullerton and USC Game Innovation Lab. 12-page PDF. https://static1.squarespace.com/static/5972908bf7e0ab1a5fe04927/t/639135c4c950f2695cfa4e2b/1670460869306/Walden_Edu_Self-Reliance_Curriculum.pdf.

GameFAQs. 2015. "Worst Game I've Ever Played: Gone Home: Console Edition." GameSpot. December 15, 2015. https://gamefaqs.gamespot.com/boards/184028-gone-home-console-edition/73036846.

Gee, James Paul. 2003. *What Video Games Have to Teach Us about Learning and Literacy*. New York: Palgrave Macmillan.

———. 2007. *Good Video Games and Good Learning: Collected Essays on Video Games Learning and Literacy*. New York: Peter Lang.

Gioia, Dana. 2007. "To Read or Not to Read." Research Report #47. Washington, DC: National Endowment for the Arts. https://www.arts.gov/sites/default/files/ToRead.pdf.

Grahame, Kenneth. 1908. *The Wind in the Willows*, New York: Charles Scribner's Sons.

Gray, Peter. 2013. *Free to Learn: Why Unleashing the Instinct to Play Will Make Our Children Happier, More Self-Reliant and Better Students for Life*. New York: Basic Books.

———. 2017. "What Exactly Is Play, and Why Is It Such a Powerful Vehicle for Learning?" *Topics in Language Disorders* 37 (3): 217–228.

Greenham, David. 2019. *Close Reading: The Basics*. London: Routledge, .

Hall, Stuart. 1973. *Encoding and Decoding in the Television Discourse*. Birmingham, UK: Centre for Cultural Studies, University of Birmingham.

"Heavy Rain (review)." 2010. *Edge*, no. 212: 88–89.

Hiemstra, Roger. 2001. "Uses and Benefits of Journal Writing." In *Promoting Journal Writing in Adult Education*, edited by L. M. English and M. A. Gillen, 19–26. New Directions for Adult and Continuing Education no. 90. San Francisco: Jossey-Bass.

Hoyt, Reed J. 1985. "Reader-Response and Implication-Realization." *Journal of Aesthetics and Art Criticism* 43 (3): 281–290.

Huizinga, Johan. 1955. *Homo Ludens: A Study of the Play-Element in Culture*. Boston: Beacon Press.

Hunicke, Robin, Marc LeBlanc, and Robert Zubek. 2004. "MDA: A Formal Approach to Game Design and Game Research." *Proceedings of the AAAI Workshop on Challenges in Game AI* (July): 25–29.

Iser, Wolfgang. 1978. *The Act of Reading: A Theory of Aesthetic Response*. Baltimore: Johns Hopkins University Press.

"iThrive Curriculum: Museum of Me 'iThrive Curriculum: Museum of Me.'" 2021. iThrive Games. Accessed 16 June, 2021. https://ithrivegames.org/ithrive-curriculum/museum-of-me/.

iThrive Games. 2019. "iThrive Curriculum: Museum of Me (Trailer)." YouTube video. 4:11. May 15, 2019. https://youtu.be/Pa5oPmQEYa4?si=4bdNLCK_xitvdvcU.

Jenkins, Henry. 2006. *Convergence Culture: Where Old and New Media Collide*. New York: New York University Press.

Joyce, James. 1920. *Ulysses*. London: Montez Press.

Juul, Jesper. 2016. *The Art of Failure: An Essay on the Pain of Playing Video Games*. Cambridge, MA: MIT Press.

Juul, Jesper, and Jason Scott Begy. 2016. "Good Feedback for Bad Players? A Preliminary Study of 'Juicy' Interface Feedback." FDG/DiGRA Conference, Dundee, UK, August, 5 2016.

Kapur, Manu. 2008. "Productive Failure." *Cognition and Instruction* 26 (3): 379–424.

Keogh, Brendan. 2012. *Killing Is Harmless: A Critical Reading of Spec Ops: The Line*. Marden, Australia: Stolen Projects.

Kesler Ted. 2018. *The Reader Response Notebook: Teaching toward Agency Autonomy and Accountability*. Urbana, IL: National Council of Teachers of English.

Kinda Funny Games. 2016. "Greg Miller's Quietest Let's Play Ever—Kinda Funny Plays That Dragon, Cancer." YouTube video, 55:50. January 15, 2016. https://www.youtube.com/watch?v=_X9OKRxlxNs.

Koster, Raph. 2004. *A Theory of Fun for Game Design*. Sebastopol, CA: O'Reilly Media.

Lantz, Frank. 2023. *The Beauty of Games*. Cambridge, MA: MIT Press.

Laurel, Brenda. 1991. Computers as Theater. Menlo Park, CA: Addison-Wesley Publishing Co.

Lennon J. Robert, and Carmen Maria Machado, eds. 2023. *Critical Hits: Writers Playing Video Games*. Minneapolis: Graywolf Press.

Lund, Nicholas. 2019. "Birding Like It's 1899: Inside a Blockbuster American West Video Game." Audubon (National Audubon Society). January 2, 2019. https://www.audubon.org/news/birding-its-1899-inside-blockbuster-american-west-video-game.

Matulef, Jeffrey. 2017. "What Remains of Edith Finch Director Ian Dallas Reflects on his Unforgettable Family Drama." Eurogamer. July 28, 2017. https://www.eurogamer.net/what-remains-of-edith-finch-director-ian-dallas-reflects-on-his-unforgettable-family-drama.

McMahon, Susan I., and Taffy Raphael. 1997. *The Book Club Connection: Literacy Learning and Classroom Talk*. New York: Teachers College Press.

Miekkob3. 2013. "Gone Home Speedrun in 47 seconds." YouTube video, 1:15. August 18, 2013. https://www.youtube.com/watch?v=p9qlm8olmn0.

Miller, Arthur. 1953. *The Crucible*. Ipswich, MA: Grey House.

Miller, Donalyn. 2013. *Reading in the Wild: The Book Whisperer's Keys to Cultivating Lifelong Reading Habits*. San Francisco: Jossey-Bass.

Milne, A. A. 1926. *Winnie-the-Pooh*. Toronto: McClelland & Stewart, Ltd.

Minotti, Mike. 2018. "How Nier: Automata Took Inspiration from a Coca-Cola Campaign." VentureBeat. March 21, 2018. https://venturebeat.com/games/how-nier-automata-took-inspiration-from-a-coca-cola-campaign/.

Montgomery, Lucy Maud. 1908. *Anne of Green Gables*. Boston: L. C. Page & Co.

Morganti, Emily. 2013. "Review for Gone Home." AdventureGamers. August 16, 2013. https://adventuregamers.com/articles/view/25075.

Murray, Janet H. 1997. *Hamlet on the Holodeck: The Future of Narrative in Cyberspace*. New York: The Free Press.

Musgrove, Laurence. 2005. "What Happens When We Read: Picturing a Reader's Responsibilities." *Journal of the Assembly for Expanded Perspectives on Learning* 11 (7) (Winter): 52–63.

New Games Foundation. 1976. *The New Games Book*. Garden City, NY: Dolphin Books.

Nicolaou, Elena. 2020. "The Best Book Club Questions to Spark Discussion." Oprah Daily. February 28, 2020.https://www.oprahdaily.com/entertainment/a31047508/book-club-questions/.

Nielson, Jakob. 2012. "Thinking Aloud: The #1 Usability Tool." Nielsen Norman Group. January 15, 2012. https://www.nngroup.com/articles/thinking-aloud-the-1-usability-tool/.

Noddings, Nel. 2003. *Caring: A Feminine Approach to Ethics and Moral Education.* 2nd ed. Berkeley: University of California Press.

———. 2012. "The Caring Relation in Teaching." *Oxford Review of Education* 38 (6): 771–781.

Nodelman, Perry. n.d. "The Pleasures of Literature" (blog). Perry Nodelman. https://perrynodelman.com/the-pleasures-of-literature/.

———. 1985. "Text as Teacher: The Beginning of *Charlotte's Web.*" *Children's Literature* 13 (1): 109–127.

Nodelman, Perry, and Mavis Reimer. 2003. *The Pleasures of Children's Literature.* 3rd ed. Boston: Allyn and Bacon.

Ouellette, Sophia. 2016. "Makers & Gamers: Journey." PlayStation. YouTube video, 10:57. March 21, 2016. https://www.youtube.com/watch?v=cxAiFuA6dz8.

Pasqualotto, Angela, Irene Altarelli, Antonella De Angeli, Zeno Menestrina, Daphne Bavelier, and Paola Venuti. 2022. "Enhancing Reading Skills through a Video Game Mixing Action Mechanics and Cognitive Training." *Nature Human Behaviour* 6 (4): 545–554.

Piaget, Jean. 1962. *Play, Dreams and Imitation in Childhood.* New York: Norton.

Plath, Sylvia. 1963. *The Bell Jar.* New York: Faber and Faber.

Poe, Edgar Allen. 1843. "Tell-Tale Heart." *The Pioneer: A Literary and Critical Magazine.* Philadelphia: Drew and Scammel.

Portman, Steve. 2020. "Reflective Journaling: A Portal into the Virtues of Daily Writing." *Reading Teacher* 73 (5): 597–602.

Posso, Alberto. 2016. "Internet Usage and Educational Outcomes among 15-Year-Old Australian Students." *International Journal of Communication* 10:3851–3876. https://ijoc.org/index.php/ijoc/article/view/5586.

Raphael, Taffy E., and Susan I. McMahon. 1994. "Book Club: An Alternative Framework for Reading Instruction." *Reading Teacher* 48 (2): 102–116.

Rosenblatt, Louise M. 1938. *Literature as Exploration.* New York: Appleton-Century.

———. 1995. *Literature as Exploration.* 5th ed. New York: Modern Language Association of America.

———. 1978. *The Reader, the Text, the Poem: The Transactional Theory of the Literary Work.* Carbondale: Southern Illinois University Press.

———. 1986. "The Aesthetic Transaction." *Journal of Aesthetic Education* 20 (4): 122–28.

Ruberg, Bo. 2017. "Playing to Lose." In *Gaming Representation: Race, Gender, and Sexuality in Video Games*, edited by Jennifer Malkowski and Treaandrea M. Russworm, 197–211. Bloomington: Indiana University Press.

Salen, Katie, and Eric Zimmerman. 2004. *Rules of Play: Game Design Fundamentals*. Cambridge, MA: MIT Press.

Sanden, Sherry, Cassandra Mattoon, and Sandra L Osorio. 2021. *Book Talk: Growing into Early Literacy through Read-Aloud Conversations*. New York: Teachers College Press.

Sanders, A. 2016. "Emotional Response to Gaming Producing Rosenblatt's Transaction." In *Emotions, Technology, and Digital Games*, edited by Sharon Y. Tettegah and David Huang Wenhao, 115–136. London: Academic Press Elsevier.

———. 2013. "Parallels Between the Gaming Experience and Rosenblatt's Reader Response Theory." PhD diss., University of North Texas. https://digital.library.unt.edu/ark:/67531/metadc271890/.

Schön, Donald A. 1983. *The Reflective Practitioner: How Professionals Think in Action*. New York: Basic Books.

Schleiner, Anne-Marie, Joan Leandre, and Brody Condon. 2002. Velvet Strike. Net Art Anthology. https://anthology.rhizome.org/velvet-strike.

Sendak, Maurice. 1963. *Where the Wild Things Are*. New York: HarperCollins.

Shakespeare, William. (1597) 1988. "Romeo and Juliet." The Complete Plays. London: The Folio Society.

———. (1611) 1988. "The Tempest." The Complete Plays. London: The Folio Society.

———. (1623) 1988. "The Tragedy Macbeth." The Complete Plays. London: The Folio Society.

———. (1623) 1988. "The Tragedy of Hamlet, Prince of Denmark." The Complete Plays. London: The Folio Society.

SinaeAzule. 2017. "[Part 3] Walden, A Game." YouTube video, 3:03:24. July 25, 2017. https://www.youtube.com/watch?v=imR8T_h95e8.

Sipe, Lawrence R. 2008. *Storytime: Young Children's Literary Understanding in the Classroom*. New York: Teachers College Press.

Smagorinsky, Peter, and Cindy O'Donnell-Allen. 1998. "Reading as Mediated and Mediating Action: Composing Meaning for Literature through Multimedia Interpretive Texts." *Reading Research Quarterly* 33 (2): 198–226.

Stevenson, Robert Louis. (1883) 1888. *Treasure Island*. Boston: Roberts Brothers.

Stang, Sarah. 2019. "'This Action Will Have Consequences': Interactivity and Player Agency." *Game Studies* 19, no. 1 (May). https://gamestudies.org/1901/articles/stang.

Sudnow, David. 1983. *Pilgrim in the Microworld*. New York: Warner Books.

Suits, Bernard. 1978. *The Grasshopper: Games, Life and Utopia*. Peterborough, ON: Broadview Press.

Sutton-Smith, Brian. 1966. "Piaget on Play: A Critique." *Psychological Review* 73 (1): 104–110.

———. 1997. *The Ambiguity of Play*. Cambridge, MA: Harvard University Press.

Swink, Steve. 2009. *Game Feel: A Game Designer's Guide to Virtual Sensation*. Amsterdam: Morgan Kaufmann Publishers/Elsevier.

Taylor, Alice. "Limbo." 2011. In Davidson 2011, 37–44.

Tekodda. 2020. "*Walden, a game* Review." Steam Community. November 11, 2020. https://steamcommunity.com/profiles/76561198409987403/recommended/1011700/.

Thoreau, Henry David. 1854. *Walden; or, life in the woods*. Boston: Ticknor and Fields.

Thorson, Maddy. 2020. "Is Madeline Canonically Trans?" Medium. November 6, 2020. https://maddythorson.medium.com/is-madeline-canonically-trans-4277ece02e40.

Trammell, Aaron. 2023. *Repairing Play: A Black Phenomenology*. Cambridge, MA: MIT Press.

Trefry, Greg. 2011. "La Noche de los Muertos." In Davidson 2011, 237–252.

Twain, Mark. 1884. *The Adventures of Huckleberry Finn*. New York: Harper & Brothers Publishers.

Upton, Brian. 2015. *The Aesthetic of Play*. Cambridge, MA: MIT Press.

———. 2017. *Situational Game Design*. London: Taylor and Francis.

Vogler, Christopher. 1992. *The Writer's Journey: Mythic Structure for Writers*. Studio City, CA: Michael Wiese Productions.

von Gillern, Sam. 2016. "The Gamer Response and Decision Framework: A Tool for Understanding Video Gameplay Experiences." *Simulation and Gaming* 47 (5): 666–683.

Vygotsky, Lev. 1967. "Play and Its Role in the Mental Development of the Child." *Soviet Psychology* 5 (3): 6–18.

———. 1978. *Mind in Society: The Development of Higher Psychological Processes*. Cambridge, MA: Harvard University Press, 1978.

White, E. B. 1952. *Charlotte's Web*. New York: Harper Trophy.

Woltmann, Suzy. 2023. "What Is Immersive Theater?" Backstage. May 8, 2023. https://www.backstage.com/magazine/article/immersive-theatre-explained-75850/.

Wright, Will. 2001. "Will Wright's Design Plunder." Game Developer Conference. YouTube video, 65:00. https://youtu.be/_Um5hfcXchU?si=JksuvWr5rXcYEHcD.

Zagal, José. 2011. "Heavy Rain—How I Learned to Trust the Designer." In Davidson 2011, 55–66.

Zillmann, Dolf. 1988. "Mood Management through Communication Choices." *American Behavioral Scientist* 31 (3): 327–340.

Index

Note: Page numbers in italics denote references to figures.